THE FEDERAL REPUBLIC OF GERMANY IN THE 1980s

Foreign Policies and Domestic Changes

Edited by
ROBERT GERALD LIVINGSTON

A Symposium with
Contributions by

Robert Gerald Livingston
Catherine McArdle Kelleher
Angela E. Stent
Stephen F. Szabo

German Information Center

A publication of the
German Information Center
410 Park Avenue
New York, N.Y. 10022

© 1983 by Robert Gerald Livingston,
Catherine McArdle Kelleher,
Angela E. Stent, and Stephen F. Szabo
ISBN: 0-912685-02-6
Library of Congress Catalog Card Number: 83-83023

Produced by Fred Weidner & Son Printers, Inc.

CONTENTS

1 An Introduction to the Federal Republic in the 1980s
Robert Gerald Livingston   1

2 The Federal Republic and NATO: Change and Continuity
Catherine McArdle Kelleher   7

3 Intra-German Relations: The View from Bonn
Angela E. Stent   19

4 The New Generation: Protest and Postmaterialism
Stephen F. Szabo   31

5 The 1983 National Elections: Three Winners and a Loser
Robert Gerald Livingston   43

1

An Introduction to the Federal Republic in the 1980s

Robert Gerald Livingston

For the United States the Federal Republic has for thirty-five years been the best of all possible Germanies. It has been steadfastly loyal to the U.S.-dominated Atlantic alliance and welcomed a large American army permanently on its soil. It has accommodated dutifully to a territorial status quo in Europe which divides the German nation and has raised no challenges to it which might test the United States' formal commitment to support German reunification.

Moreover, Germans generally share Americans' respect for a free market economy, for a liberal international trading order, and for the influence of business in society and politics. Encouraged initially by American occupation re-educators, the Germans have developed a multiparty democracy which provides for smooth and comfortably infrequent changes of government. Unlike other important allies such as the French or Italians, they have relegated their communist party to insignificance and have, except for a few brief years in the 1960s, given no support to far right or neo-Nazi parties either. They appear devoted to the values which we Americans like to stand for in the world. They have actually "Americanized" their way of life to a greater degree than any other country except conceivably Canada.

For all that, Americans interested in European affairs remain constantly uneasy about the Germans and where they might be going. The Federal Republic's economic, political and military weight and its key strategic position mean that change in its political orientation would have a powerful effect on the international order. Doubts keep arising about the Germans' real loyalty to NATO, an alliance which, it is often forgotten, was constructed to guard as much against a resurgent Germany as against an aggressive Russia. Will Bonn do as other German governments have done in the past, make a deal with the Russians—this time to insure closer relations with the German Democratic Republic (GDR), the Soviet Union's subservient ally, with the long-term aim of unifying the nation politically again? Worries are also growing about the values and allegiance of West German youth. For the first time in over 25 years, a political party, supported mainly by the young, opposed to the Atlantic alliance and in favor of neutralism, is now represented in the *Bundestag*. Such questions, although perennially posed about the Federal Republic, have taken on a new urgency in the 1980s, when the West Germans have regained self-confidence and enhanced their international room for maneuver. In March 1983 they elected a government that is in the strongest position of any since the war. How will it use its strength? In ways that are familiar to Americans and fully in keeping with our own foreign policy objectives?

Four topics which relate to such questions are treated in the following chapters, which grew out of a seminar arranged in May 1983 by the Smithsonian Institution's Resident Associate Program in collaboration with its Woodrow Wilson International Center for Scholars. Entitled "West Germany in Transition," the seminar was organized in conjunction with celebrations of the tricentennial (1683–1983) of German immigration to America. The first two chapters deal with foreign policy issues: on the Federal Republic and NATO by Catherine McArdle Kelleher and on relations between West and East Germany by Angela E. Stent. The second set, on the attitudes of young Germans by Stephen F. Szabo and on the outcome of the 1983 national elections, have a domestic policy focus but also point to trends that will have direct policy implications for the Federal Republic's relationship with the United States.

Two common threads appear in all of the chapters. First is the assumption that the Federal Republic of the 1980s will be more vigorous in asserting its national interests. Beginning with Willy Brandt's *Ostpolitik* (Eastern Policy) more than a decade ago, West Germany began to come into its own internationally. This necessarily entails a certain distancing from the United States. Second is the probability that the Germans, having become less deferential to authority and elite decision-making, will be more actively concerned with foreign policy and national security issues. Professors Kelleher and Stent remain cautious in their predictions of the consequences: it is their view that the Federal

Republic can find no better structure to insure its security than NATO and that opportunities for new political relationships with the East, specifically with East Germany, remain inherently limited. Professor Szabo's analysis points out the more critical attitudes about the United States that prevail among Germans born since 1945, whose values in many respects differ widely from those of their elders. The spread of the West German peace movement and the unexpected success of the Green Party in the March 1983 election suggest that such attitudes are gaining political strength.

West Germans' support for NATO and the United States remains very high, notwithstanding these new attitudes among youth. The election results, which gave the clearly pro-NATO and pro-U.S. party, the Christian Democrats/Christian Social Union (CDU/CSU)*, a resounding victory, confirm this. Germans seem to share Professor Kelleher's view that NATO and the U.S. defense guarantee will continue to provide the best security option for the Federal Republic for the foreseeable future. Partly this is true because Germany's strength is so great and its role in the alliance so crucial that it is able to use NATO effectively to influence the policies of other members, including the United States.

The German goverment and public are, however, questioning much more closely today than at any time in the last twenty years the costs and benefits to them of alliance bargains struck during the 1950s. They see the United States continuously seeking more from its NATO partners, in areas outside of Europe for instance, than Germany is willing to give. Controversies about a fair sharing of alliance burdens and costs persist. Recurrent doubts in Bonn about the predictability and reliability of United States policies became pronounced during the Carter and Reagan administrations and now color all Bonn's foreign policy decisions. Fears that the Americans are going to abandon the Federal Republic and revert to some kind of isolationism are endemic. But it seems no less true in the 1980s than it was in the 1950s that "the only possible choice" remains the choice for NATO and the West. Reunification options, in this view, may have looked worth exploring in the 1950s, but they will not be actively considered during the 1980s.

Reunification does remain the ultimate goal, however. For that reason relations between the two Germanies, the Federal Republic and the German Democratic Republic, deserve great attention. Professor

---

*At many places in this book where no confusion can arise, "Christian Democrats" is used when both the CDU and its Bavarian sister party the CSU, which together form a single parliamentary group, are meant. "Germany" is used similarly in place of The Federal Republic of Germany.

Stent finds in fact that intra-German relations indirectly constitute "... the most important source of U.S.-West German tensions over East-West relations today." For reunification and for any major steps toward it the Federal Republic remains dependent on the Soviet Union, the United States' adversary. Americans forget this elemental fact of German politics and foreign policy. Because of it, the Federal Republic is always reluctant to follow an American initiative if it looks as if it would lead to confrontation with the Soviets. For Bonn the effort to expand intercourse with East Germany has become a "cornerstone of *Deutschlandpolitik*" (policy relating to Germany as a whole, especially toward the GDR). Bonn's hesitation to support Washington's moves against the Soviet Union in the wake of the invasion of Afghanistan in 1979 or when martial law was imposed in Poland in 1981 should have made the connections amply clear.

Bonn's short-term objectives in its dealings with the GDR are modest: to multiply contacts between families, ease travel restrictions, and maintain trade and other economic relations. Such aims are of primary concern to Germans but do not attract great attention, much less enthusiasm, abroad. Consequently their political importance to Bonn tends to be discounted in other countries. Professor Stent believes that reunification interests only a small minority of Germans today, mostly on the far left and right, but that improvement of ties with the GDR has "considerable importance to the electorate." Little change in the importance or the nature of intra-German relations will occur in the 1980s, she predicts. Nevertheless, Bonn cannot be expected to reduce efforts to expand these ties even if its effort does not seem to be inducing change in East Germany—the original justification for the *Ostpolitik* and *Deutschlandpolitik* launched during the 1960s.

Disturbing questions crop up when the Federal Republic's *Deutschlandpolitik* is examined. What benefits to the West arise from unsettling or destabilizing the GDR, something which is quite likely to result from closer relations with its vastly more powerful, attractive and self-assured western neighbor? Professor Stent is convinced that East Germany's fears of such influence impose a strict limit on how far it will go in moving closer to the Federal Republic. Can the two Germanies insulate their relationship from rivalry between the superpowers? There have been signs recently that both want to do so. What then if this leads the relationship to develop its own dynamic? And finally, does the United States fully realize that the West Germans count on it as an ally to support their pursuit of this special national interest?

Young Germans at least, as Professor Szabo points out, have very different expectations of the United States than their parents had.

They are more critical of the country which was, as Günter Grass has commented, the West Germans' "ersatz fatherland" for many years after World War II. Those born since 1945, however, have had no experience with the crises that brought the wartime enemies together so quickly—the Marshall Plan, the Berlin Blockade, and the Cold War against communism. America is no fatherland to them.

Those under 25 in particular, many of whom are supporters of the peace movement and the Green Party, have become disillusioned with all "establishment" institutions, the United States and the Atlantic alliance included. Their values do not relate to defense against communism, economic growth, individual achievement or material acquisition. Their concerns are rather peace, quality of life, the environment, and other "postmaterialist" issues. Professor Szabo leaves open the question of young people's national aspirations. It is clear that they think no better of the Soviet and the East German system than they do of the American. Some other observers do detect nationalist inclinations in the attempt of the West German peace movement to establish links with a small and courageous counterpart in the GDR. Professor Stent, however, believes that interest in relationships with East Germany may generally wane in the 1980s, as political power in the Federal Republic is assumed by a generation which has had no experience with the unified German state that existed until 1945.

Young Germans in the Green Party are not political dropouts. Quite the contrary. They call for a broadening of political participation. And like Germans in the past they are cause-oriented. Were German reunification to become a cause with prospects, is it not likely that the politically active young would take it up?

The 1983 elections provided few answers, even by inference, to questions of this kind. Fought mainly on economic issues, they gave the CDU/CSU, which called for a "vote for recovery," a solid victory. For the electorate, the Christian Democrats stand for good relations with the Americans and with the alliance. Their 49 percent vote demonstrated NATO's popular support. The big losers last March were the Social Democrats (SPD), who won only slightly over 38 percent. The voters held them responsible for the economic downturn and unemployment of the last few years. The SPD also appeared indecisive on the only foreign policy issue in the elections, the scheduled stationing of new American medium-range missiles (Pershing II and cruise) in the Federal Republic. The Christian Democrats succeeded in depicting this SPD equivocation as opposition to NATO.

With less than six percent of the vote, the Greens, the party of the young subculture which Professor Szabo examines, do not look formidable. They won only 27 seats in the 498-member *Bundestag*. Their modest success is more surprising and perhaps indicative of the future than it first appears. Not since 1957 has a party other than the traditional three—CDU/CSU, SPD, and the liberal FDP (Free Democratic Party)—made it into the parliament. The Greens' success legitimizes the party and provides it with new impetus, platforms, and financial support from the state. It is also influencing the much larger Social Democratic Party to adopt some of the Greens' issues, in an effort to absorb them. This aim explains why the SPD in late 1983 voted against deployment of the Pershing and cruise missiles on German territory. It is possible too that the Social Democrats will now move toward some of the positions which they advocated in the 1950s, such as zones free of nuclear weapons or foreign troops and perhaps even modification of the Federal Republic's NATO role.

The government which Chancellor Kohl formed after the elections has stressed continuity in the Federal Republic's foreign policy, toward the West especially but also toward the East and the GDR. The Chancellor has made a particular effort to establish warm relations with President Reagan, who also heads an administration that is right of center. With a solid majority and great strength at national, state and local levels, the Christian Democrats find themselves powerfully positioned. Their tenure in office will last for the rest of the decade, if the past glacial rate of change in German politics is any indication. Today's political constellation may recall the 1950s at first glance—a dominant CDU/CSU, a weak SPD and several minor parties. But today's German voters, among whom the number of young will bulk relatively larger as the decade progresses, are quite different from the outcast, disoriented and apprehensive Germans of the 1950s. They are less willing than Germans of thirty years ago to intone "Ja und Amen" to all American foreign policies. The Federal Republic of the 1980s, one may contend, is a more valuable ally not only because it is stronger and more confident but also because it is more mature and critical. American policymakers' understanding of German interests will be severely tested during the 1980s and must prove sophisticated if we are to preserve our past close alignment with this best of all possible Germanies.

2

The Federal Republic and NATO: Change and Continuity in the 1980s

Catherine McArdle Kelleher

To discuss Germany and NATO in the 1980s is both the easiest and the most risk-fraught task of any symposium. At issue are a set of relationships, primarily German-American ties, which have been the critical forces in shaping the Federal Republic as we know it today. In the judgment of many—both Germans and Americans—the present NATO security arrangements consitute the best framework Germany could hope for in the coming decade. On the questions that matter most to Germans, and particularly to German political, military and economic elites, Bonn now has the say of a major world power. It possesses assets which allow it to influence significantly the policy outcomes for all Western states, including the United States. To put it simply, it cannot always secure what a totally independent policy might attempt, but it can almost always prevent unwanted or disadvantageous decisions within NATO or its bilateral relationships.

The question of the moment is the stability of these relations and how they might evolve. At the moment there is much superficial talk of an "Atlantic crisis," of threats to the existing NATO framework. Most of this talk is overblown. But there are significant winds of change throughout the West, most especially within Germany and the United States. How easy will it be to maintain the present state of relationships? How much flexibility and re-equalizing effort will be needed to offset the greater strain, the greater diversity, and the continuing mutual irritation which the 1980s seem to promise?

Much of the answer will be found in Bonn as a new leadership generation and a maturing political system grow in power and responsibility. But at least an equal measure will depend on what happens in the United States. How will the United States, and the leaders elected in the 1980s, manage the problem of normalizing the security relationship with Bonn?

The argument here is that the present debate should not be viewed as an isolated event or a disagreement over a specific set of policies. Rather it is simply a stage of a necessary readjustment both countries are going through as they re-evaluate their security agendas and priorities. The Federal Republic in particular is now a significant global actor, able and willing to fight for its interests and the role it wishes to play. Its achievements are notable in many areas—as the economic seminars held by Helmut Schmidt for successive American presidents pointed up.

Security and arms control is the last area of readjustment because it is the most important—for Germany, for the United States and for the European balance. The problems of final "normalization" may benefit from occasional periods of benign neglect and even from regular public review of what has already been achieved. But the issue of what is significant and necessary change from the perspective of both countries will neither go away nor allow serenity in the decade to come.

THE CORE: THE GERMAN-AMERICAN SECURITY RELATIONSHIP

For the present and for the future, the stakes involved in the German-American security relationship are remarkably clear. In most significant respects, this is the dominant alliance relationship for both; each is and almost surely will remain the most important ally of the other. For Americans, it is almost odd to acknowledge this fact. For Germans there is no question. Both states have an enormous investment in their common NATO security effort made over nearly thirty years—whether one measures it in terms of military costs, commitment of manpower, or percentage of GNP devoted to their NATO "share." Bilaterally, there has also been a continuous undergirding of the security relationship with a healthy set of economic ties.

A subject of great controversy among voters in both countries in the 1980s is the question of the net costs and benefits of this relationship. In the interest of long-term security, West Germany is said to have given the United States not just the lead, but the dominant role in defining what constitutes its national security, and what is the best way to pursue it. For young Germans, in particular, the issue most simply defined is whether German security policy has not been made largely of, by, and for the United States.

The answer to this question is a simple "yes." The starting point is the crucial role the United States played in the process of rearmament, of Germany's admission as a full NATO member less than a decade after defeat. Most significant now is the lead, if not the overwhelming influence, exercised by the United States in determining what will be done if German territory is attacked. The peacetime presence of large numbers of Americans, more than 500,000 troops and dependents, on German soil is unprecedented. Fifty years ago, the maintenance outside the continental borders of a standing army of 200,000 men with permanent installations would have been grounds for grave concern, if not for presidential impeachment, in many parts of the United States. Today these are accepted figures in the American political landscape. Moreover, the forces bear with them awesome weapons of nuclear destruction—in the thousands, on German soil, under American control and subject to decisions made by an American president.

Voters in the United States, or at least those interested in foreign policy, ask the logical follow-on: What difference does it all make? Is West Germany now doing its fair share—in terms of money, manpower, or even responsibility for the hard choices to be made? Is it willing to take on new responsibilities commensurate with its global economic role and advantageous to the United States as American postwar preeminence diminishes? What is it now that Germans really want in terms of NATO structure and doctrines, in relations with the Soviet Union or in containing conflicts in the Third World? And what are they prepared to pay for?

Confusion is evident on both sides of the Atlantic as to just what the German side of this security relationship has been. For at least fifteen years, the Federal Republic has been the principal partner of the United States in NATO. It has outranked the other allies on key dimensions—in the contribution of ground forces, in absolute levels of money spent, in standing capabilities and mobilization potential. Germany has played roles of similar significance in determining the direction and shape of NATO affairs. This has been true whether German influence has been felt through the very intense, often fractious, always important, bilateral relationship with the U.S. or through more formal channels within NATO or the military leadership.

This is a role which, almost every student of Germany would argue, has enjoyed considerable popular support. Every public opinion poll in the postwar period has recorded high levels of German public approval for the alliance and its activities. Clearly, the present debate in Germany involves articulate, often impassioned critiques which suggest all this has changed. But most observers suggest that NATO still enjoys the support of the German "silent majority." If the Soviets would once again rescue NATO from itself by fomenting a crisis, if the direct question of membership were again to be struck, a fairly certain prediction would be German support, if not enthusiasm, for the integration of German and general Western security under NATO.

It should also not be forgotten that Germany's NATO role has come only after a long set of debates within each of the major political parties. The first decade of rearmament, 1950—1960, was the most dramatic. In election after election, at the local and at the national level, the symbolic debate at least was about what the future of Germany should be. The focus in part was on what is often referred to as the "myth" of lost opportunities. A number of German leaders, most from the SPD but others too, stressed the opportunities that the Soviets on three occasions seemed to present for reunification on acceptable terms. The condition was that Germany was not to rearm or enter the Western alliance. Whether the lost opportunities were real opportunities or merely very good propaganda points is something which only a very detailed discussion could answer. The price—a neutral Germany, reunited but without forces of its own—was one which very few West Germans and even fewer West Europeans were prepared to pay. Certainly, successive American administrations—Truman and Eisenhower—were unwilling to have the Germans pay that price. In the end, that may well have been the decisive factor.

There were, however, others who saw the solution best in a European framework. Konrad Adenauer, the first postwar chancellor, has to be counted among them at least in the early years of the decade. European security, rather than German security, was to be the framework in which the questions of how to defend Germany would be resolved. The defeat in 1954 of the European Defense Community— the basic British-French-German agreement that was necessary to sustain any European framework—meant that, for Adenauer, NATO became the only possible choice.

His calculation reveals his set of solutions to the "German question" that had been plaguing the European order since 1870. German security was in fact going to be dependent on two very basic principles for at least the next several decades. First, it would be dependent on the direct involvement of the United States in European security. The United States was not only the most powerful state to be mobilized in defense of European security. It was also the only nation that could both balance European fears and resentments against Germany and secure German rearmament, with a pledge of good behavior, on terms under which such rearmament would be acceptable as well as necessary within the security framework of the West. A second principle was that Germany would participate only on the basis of full rehabilitation and equal treatment. There would, for example, be no surrender of German territory in the event of conflict; at least in terms of basic political commitment and preconflict rhetoric, there would be no retreat to the Rhine or perhaps to the west of the Rhine if and when a Soviet invasion would occur. Germans slowly but surely would be given full recognition in terms of their role and influence in Western security planning.

It would only be then that West Germany might explore other solutions to the questions of German national identity. If the Germans were strong enough vis-à-vis the Soviet Union to compel unification on acceptable terms, they would be important enough vis-à-vis the rest of the West to make sure whatever future option was available would be one that would be respected by the other countries as well. (One can only speculate about what Adenauer's motives were and what his personal timetable looked like.)

Much of the second decade of rearmament, from 1960 to 1970, can be discussed as a successive set of crises about how much equity Germany was due within NATO. At times, it was a flexing of German muscle to be met often with a critical U.S. or French response (particularly under DeGaulle) which would then lead to a solution not precisely on lines wished for by Bonn. The list of particular disputes with the United States was long. Perhaps the most important debate was about the shift to a strategy of so-called flexible response (1961 – 1967). At least from the German perspective, that strategy would allow the prospect that a conventional war, and perhaps even a tactical nuclear war, would be limited to German soil. Indeed, the first line of Western defense would be a conflict on German soil which would either allow time for negotiation or force the choice of escalation on the aggressor himself. As Germans of the period were sometimes heard to say, "Whether it's conventional or nuclear, or whether it's limited from someone else's vantage point, we'll all be dead anyway."

Another, less often discussed issue was U.S. pressure on the Germans during 1965 and 1966 to emulate the Korean War model and to become directly involved in the Vietnam War. In the view of the Johnson administration, and of successive administrations, the issue of security for Europe did not begin and end within a European framework. It was the responsibility of the Germans also to shoulder some of the global burden. Quite apart from the fact that President Johnson had overlooked certain key provisions of the German constitution, the role was rejected by the German government as being politically unacceptable and as beyond their capacity in terms of the search for equity.

In other issues with the United States, Bonn took similar critical stances but ended, more often than not, with a solution that was at least acceptable to both sides, if more often weighted towards U.S. interests. One example is a successive number of economic crises in the 1960s, ending with the German recession of the mid-60s and the curtailing of direct offset payments for the costs of U.S. troops stationed on German territory. The bargain was struck that these payments would not end in the mid-60s, but that they would be revised and stretched out, and would indeed end at a later point in the 1970s. It was a bargain which, in fact, the Germans were then able to turn more or less to their advantage.

The 1970s to the 1980s saw the emergence of Germany as the critical NATO partner. It became the partner not only to be heard on a specific issue or in a specific crisis, and not only to assert its own positions vis-à-vis those of the United States. It was the European interlocutor—with both the power and the capacity to explain to the United States, often in detail, just precisely what the issues of European-American controversy were. During the 1973 Arab-Israeli war, the Germans refused automatic extension of overflight rights, and the resupply of the Israeli forces from American stocks held on German territory. This came as a shock to many in the American political elite. Similarly, Bonn was critical of the actual content of the SALT II Treaty in 1976 and 1977, and equally critical in 1979 and 1980 of the American failure to ratify that treaty. There was also a far larger and more active German role in all decisions taken within NATO, whether about specific military issues such as increased readiness and buildup, the new deep strike doctrine question, host nation support, or even the particular modalities that would accompany INF (the Intermediate Nuclear Force deployment of Pershing and cruise missiles). The Federal Republic's status as critical partner by 1980 meant the assured status to talk on any and all topics, to make its role felt, and even, however burdensome and irritating equity may be, to be accorded the right to disagree on issues of significance to both countries (e.g., the pipeline, nuclear export, arms control, negotiating positions, and trade with the Soviet Union).

THE ROOTS OF CHANGE

What are the factors now that bring into question the fulfillment of the goals set forward by Adenauer, and by successive generations of German political leaders and political elites from all sectors of society? There is no single clear-cut factor that will make things change. It is really a question of how much and how well both countries turn their attention to the question of adaptation.

The concerns of Americans about future German-American relations need only brief mention here. At the simplest level there is what has been called "The Founding Fathers' Syndrome." It is the conviction that the Germans have somehow lost their way; that they have rejected the patrimony that was given to them with such care and at such cost. In a sense, the Greens are viewed as the "last straw": they are proof that Germans are too idealistic, too contrary, or too confused to fight even in their own defense. A more serious set of concerns is born of what are seen as German misunderstandings. The younger generation (and by extension, all Germans) seem now to misunderstand the nature of the historical dynamic that shaped the founding of the Federal Republic. They seem to believe they can "have it all" as a matter of right: strong alliance with the United States yet independent economic relations with the East; insured domestic social welfare as well as necessary defense spending; an American shield outside of Europe yet the freedom to criticize American foreign policy.

A second, dominant theme is burden sharing and the fair share to be paid by Germany and the other NATO states in the years ahead. The perception is widespread among American elites and mass publics that the United States is already bearing an inequitable share, and that with every new challenge it takes on an even greater burden. The Persian Gulf security commitment of the United States is seen as largely to secure European oil supplies, to insure both economic and military security for the West as a whole. How long will it be before a more equitable burden sharing formula is found? And why must the United States respect the domestic political contraints Bonn faces, while being criticized for Congressional restrictions or electoral rhetoric?

The uncertainties the Germans feel about the United States are not necessarily new, but certainly far more intense and far more openly observable than has been true in the past. Perhaps the last comparable experience was German uncertainty and confusion in the period of 1961 – 1962 over the strategy shift by the United States. What has changed now is the emergence of fears, even at the elite level, of the nearness of conflict, the possibility of Soviet-American collision. The question is whether or not the United States can be expected to react responsibly at times of crisis. It is a combination of fears that the United States will react too quickly or more probably not at all, given strategic parity with the Soviet Union. In this evolving strategic situation, Germans ask what are the controls that a German government has over what will ultimately be the course of conflict conducted on its territory. It is both fear of abandonment and fear of implementation expressed with a stridency not heard for twenty years, and by segments of the population never before mobilized on these issues.

Germans also suffer almost as much as Americans from the American post-Vietnam and post-Watergate syndromes. How is it possible to have confidence in a political system which seems to experience wild swings of public opinion, which features as a regular characteristic on-the-job training in foreign policy for its president and indeed has as its Congress a group of actors who only occasionally remember foreign policy and then in the worst possible light? The American system seemed a model of responsiveness and responsibility in the postwar decade and seemed a "good model" to replace several from German history already discarded or badly tarnished. It now appears discredited in terms of efficiency, effectiveness and even responsiveness.

This seems all the more frightening given the global scope most Germans see as the real framework of American foreign policy. They see themselves as a regional power, having different interests particularly in terms of the degree of threat perceived elsewhere in the world to factors that will affect European security. The Middle East is again the clearest example. In many senses, despite the changes in force structure that have taken place over the last couple of years, West Germans at least view U.S. actions in establishing the commitment to the security of the Persian Gulf as being a negative factor or perhaps even a subtraction from their own security. The expectation is that if conflict begins in the Middle East, one of two "bad" outcomes will occur. One is that resources necessary for European security will be diverted to that area and will not return. Alternatively, either the Soviet or the American side will have an interest in spreading conflict from the Middle East to the place where it still really matters: Central Europe. Younger Germans at least feel exposed to what they see as a set of global calculations on the part of an often unreliable United States that may make the American guarantee to treat German security as its own a sham.

These concerns about the United States and about its willingness or ability to deliver on past promises come at a time in which there is a second new set of factors: new economic realities which trouble this particular relationship to a degree not previously seen. The series of short-term arrangements (some have called them band-aids) that have been applied to the international economic arena and particularly to the interdependent policies of advanced industrial countries are, if not totally unstuck, in the process of disintegrating. The question now comes of long-term competition between the advanced industrial societies and more specifically the degree of diplomatic acrobatics that will be necessary to maintain military cooperation at a time of increasing competitiveness in global markets.

The German economic miracle that many of us thought so dominant in the 1960s has settled into a more stable, lower level of growth. Because of insufficient investment in research and development, particularly in the area of high technology, a number of German economic leaders now face the problem of declining competitiveness. There are pressures in Germany for the alleviation of the present level of unemployment (10 percent in 1983), much of which threatens to become structural. Bonn faces a high probability of continuing unemployment, perhaps involving whole generations, at levels that have always been thought politically unacceptable given the German experience in the 1920s. Because of the heavy simultaneous investment in an industrial plant, the Germans also face the problem of block obsolesence.

In short, the 1980s will be a difficult time economically and a period in which the number of cards the Germans will hold, at least in the next four or five years, is considerably fewer than they held in the 1970s, or certainly in the 1960s. Moreover, the political leadership will have increasing difficulty explaining why defense budgets must go up, if indeed unemployment continues at high levels and the demand for social welfare services therefore not only continues but grows. German elites will increasingly question why the high technology equipment, weapons, support forces, even some of the basic stocks must be purchased from American producers in order to satisfy domestic American agendas at a time when jobs in all industries in Germany are declining.

A third major factor causing concern among Germans (but Americans as well) is something which might be called the domesticization, or perhaps more aptly, the "democratization" of the security debate. It is in fact a debate which perhaps need not have happened. It was very badly handled in the mid-1970s, when it first began, by a set of German leaders who did not wish to have the details of particular security arrangements—certainly not of the storage of nuclear weapons or how they would be used—discussed by a public which might then have become even more anxious than it was already. It was far easier to say the security arrangements were matters for the elite; that these arrangements were things which somehow were forced upon them by the United States and to which they agreed reluctantly; that Germany didn't ask many questions since ultimately it was interested in deterrence and the American guarantee that backed up that deterrence, rather than the actual conduct of any conflict in Europe, which was unthinkable.

The "governmental stonewalling" of 1977 and 1978 is now past and there is far more interest and far more information dispersed far more broadly than has ever before been true in the history of the Federal Republic. Even in the time of the last great antinuclear movement—that of the late 1950s—there certainly was not a widespread knowledge of details such as the rate at which Soviet missiles are being produced, or the numbers of American nuclear weapon sites on German soil, or the degree to which American weapons, if moved in a certain direction, would be able to hit Soviet leadership targets.

The question for Americans, as for the German elite, is the impact of these changes on German political responsibility in security decision making. How is this democratization of the security debate going to affect long-term policy? In some senses, simply because of the psychological burden involved, it is clear that the present level of mass organization, of mobilization for demonstrations against nuclear weapons, is probably not going to be sustained. Psychologically, at least, it is very difficult for anyone to contemplate nuclear catastrophe involving the loss of his own life, his family, or his homeland. This is particularly true at a point when the capacity for individual influence seems either too limited or fruitless, since it cannot bring any change in the basic armament balance.

What makes this pattern different from the late 1950s, however, is that there is institutional involvement at a level that has not been true before. Churches have brought this topic into parish studies, and there is now a German pastoral letter which is parallel to (although different from) the pastoral letter produced either by American bishops, or Dutch bishops, or even Italian bishops, all representing a new institutional foundation and indeed a stake in the carrying on of the debate. The dissemination of information to schools, while still not perhaps at the level that many think necessary in a responsible democracy, American or German, is certainly far greater in the last two years than it had been at any previous point. What this democratization will mean politically, therefore, will turn on the degree to which these critical attitudes focus only on nuclear issues or are extended to a larger range of security questions. At a minimum, these questions would include those now raised in Britain: the continued stationing on German soil of American forces and American weapons, the issues of guns vs. butter, and the use of arms sales to promote diplomatic influence, to mention only a few of those in a possible German catalogue.

All of these forces for change, however, are concerned with the future, not the present. In one sense, they are anticipations of problems, projections perhaps of "worst case scenarios." At the most, carried to their logical extremes, they point towards gradual attrition of present relationships. However unsatisfactory and worrisome NATO relationships appear, the degree of popular support for the alliance and for sharing the security burden is extremely high. The present pattern, therefore, appears stable for at least the next four or five years, and is perhaps the only relevant horizon for the present Western political leaders, conservative or liberal.

FUTURE OPTIONS

The query still remains: given that the United States does not go home, and that the American political system still does support a broad NATO commitment, is it possible that there are alternative options for the organization of its security that West Germany might like to explore, either within the NATO framework of ultimately in opposition to it? One option which has been around for some time but which has been a subject of renewed interest, particularly in the last year, is a revival of the European framework for defense. It would involve not the model European Defense Community concept of the 1950s, but rather something closer perhaps to Kennedy's "two-pillar concept," with a European organization perhaps only loosely tied together and paralleling something similar on this side of the Atlantic. These two pillars would be sufficient for deterrence and in the event of war would then coalesce into a single integrated organization. Here one runs up against the same problems which were decisive in the 1950s: What is the basic willingness of Britain and France to accord Germany an equal role in such an organization, quite apart from the new problems of control which assume ever-increasing importance as the British and French forces modernize towards the 1990s and their third stage of nuclear weapons development? Would Germany in fact be protected any better, if at all, by a British and French guarantee of its security? It presumably still would not allow Britain and France a direct role in determining whether or not nuclear weapons are used in its own defense.

A second set of options, particularly consistent with the kind of economic and demographic constraints Germany will increasingly face, emphasizes a drastic change in the kind of defense organization and level of effort Germany would make. It might be a force structure that was "made in Germany," and not in the United States. It might involve perhaps cadre divisions which could be filled out with sufficient warning or greater emphasis on the use of reserves, perhaps something on the faded Swiss model of the gun and the uniform in the closet. NATO as an overarching organization would be of lesser importance, while bilateral U.S.-German ties would be crucial. The only problem is that this is a concept that includes political responsibilities and the willingness of others to go beyond some rather bad memories of the past. The use of reserves not just by Hitler, but indeed by the German leadership in the 1920s, suggests parallels in circumventing the present NATO-West European Union restrictions which were designed previously to limit Germany's control over its own security options. Again the question of the confidence of others—Europeans, Russians, and Americans—is paramount.

These are but two possibilities; there are many others that could be and have been considered. To most conceivable German leadership groups over the next decade, all of them will probably look less attractive as future options than the basic NATO framework that exists at the moment. This celebration of the status quo may be simply a tribute to the limitations of imagination in thinking of the number of events and changes that may occur. It reflects the basic continuity of German interests, the set of beliefs and calculations which have always made the Atlantic tie and the search for full equity the cornerstones of postwar German foreign policy. The dissatisfactions have grown; the probabilities for startling future achievements or new initiatives now seem very low. Yet along the crucial dimensions, it will almost certainly seem the safest bet, the policy stance which promises the fewest risks and the greatest number of future benefits, while preserving present benefits.

Still open, however, are major questions which turn on decisions and indeed even the priority of attention given to European and especially German-American issues by American administrations. How much strain will there be in normalization and adaptation? How much difficulty is there on America's part in according the final vestiges of equity promised so long ago to the Germans? And how much longer will the bargains struck in the 1950s still be fully understood by the political leaderships which will yet come to power in the 1980s and the 1990s in the United States?

3

Intra-German Relations: The View from Bonn

Angela E. Stent

The intra-German relationship is perhaps the most important source of U.S.-West German tensions over East-West relations today. Germany is a divided nation. Since the Soviet Union holds the key to improved contacts between the Federal Republic of Germany and the German Democratic Republic, the Federal Republic inevitably has a continuing interest in maintaining a dialogue with the U.S.S.R. no matter how frosty ties between Washington and Moscow become. Indeed, the Soviet Union's greatest importance for West Germany lies not in the potential direct gain of the bilateral relationship, but in the indirect benefit that the Federal Republic's *Ostpolitik* has brought its *Deutschlandpolitik*. Without Moscow, Bonn cannot hope to improve ties with East Berlin. The Federal Republic is the only Western country that has a continuing interest in an East European country. There is no other relationship in the world remotely like this. Under the new West German government, relations between the two Germanies initially appeared to have deteriorated, culminating in East German Party leader Erich Honecker's cancellation of his proposed visit to the Federal Republic, but they have recently improved again since Bonn granted a new billion-Mark loan guarantee to the GDR. Indeed, intra-German relations have experienced a number of fluctuations during the decade since the signing of the intra-German Basic Treaty in 1972. Yet despite these changing relationships, it is clear that the desire to maintain contacts between the two Germanies will remain a fundamental aspect of West German domestic and foreign policy for the rest of this century, irrespective of which party is in power.

This West German policy will always be of concern to the U.S. and its allies. Yet the U.S. interest in the intra-German relationship is not without paradoxes. NATO was formed to implement a double containment policy—to contain Germany as much as the Soviet Union; yet NATO has been officially committed to German reunification since West Germany entered the alliance. One might indeed question the extent to which either the U.S. or its other allies in practice support this goal; yet this support was the price they paid for securing the Federal Republic in the Western alliance. The U.S. is therefore committed to encouraging the intra-German dialogue, even though this very relationship has been a source of considerable German reluctance to follow the U.S. in questioning detente and adopting a more confrontational stance toward the U.S.S.R. in the last five years. These are the inherent dilemmas in U.S. relations with the Federal Republic.

This chapter will examine the past record of intra-German relations and the implications for future U.S. policy by discussing five aspects of the problem: the evolution of German policy prior to the 1969 SPD-FDP coalition; the expectations of the *Deutschlandpolitik* of the Brandt-Scheel government; the German evaluation of the results of this policy over the past decade; the current situation under the Kohl-Genscher government; and the future choices for U.S. policy.

BEFORE THE THAW: INTRA-GERMAN RELATIONS PRIOR TO 1969

During the Federal Republic's first twenty years, there were two basic approaches toward intra-German relations, which persist into the 1980s. One was always a minority view, and remains so today: the difference is that the protagonists of these views have shifted since the 1950s. The minority view in the early years of the Republic was held by the Social Democratic Party (SPD), which became the champion of German nationalism and reunification. In the 1950s, the SPD opposed the country's integration into the Western alliance, because it argued this would preclude the possibility of German reunification. The party's 1959 plan for Germany, for instance, proposed a reunified, neutralized German state, plus a neutral Poland and Czechoslovakia. Many of these early SPD ideas have recently been revived outside of the mainstream of the SPD; indeed they have never completely died. But the SPD abandoned its opposition to integration into the West after its 1959 Bad Godesberg program. It realized that its platform on intra-German ties would not bring it the needed votes. Nevertheless, there has always been a minority current of left-wing nationalism in the Federal Republic, and this survives today.

Chancellor Adenauer, by contrast, chose *Westpolitik* over *Ostpolitik*, and recognized that the country's future security lay with the Western alliance. Although his declaratory policy was heavily oriented toward the importance of German reunification, operationally he was not much committed to it. Through his insistence on the Hallstein Doctrine, whereby the Federal Republic asserted the right to speak for the whole of Germany and refused to maintain diplomatic relations with any nation that recognized the GDR, and through his refusal to deal with the "Soviet Occupation Zone," Adenauer pursued a "Policy of Strength" which excluded most direct dealings with what was designated an illegitimate state. Yet even as staunch a supporter of the U.S. as Adenauer could not entirely neglect the intra-German question. In 1958, he secretly proposed to Soviet Ambassador Smirnov that East Germany be neutralized and given the status of Austria, and subsequently he proposed a ten-year period during which East Germany would be liberalized, after which elections to decide the issue of reunification would be held. Khrushchev rejected these proposals because they did not involve any West German recognition of a communist East Germany.

During Adenauer's last year in office and the administration of his successor, the government's *Ostpolitik* became more flexible; yet there was little movement on the intra-German question. The opposition SPD tried to adopt new tactics on an inter-party level, offering an exchange of speakers with the East German communist party, the SED, in 1966, but the proposal foundered on SED opposition. It was only when Willy Brandt became foreign minister in 1966 that Bonn's *Ostpolitik* became somewhat less rigid, with the Hallstein Doctrine abandoned in 1967. Yet this more flexible policy only achieved meager results, because it did not directly address the question of West German recognition of the GDR. Ultimately, neither of the major parties in the Federal Republic was able to improve relations with the GDR or bring the two Germanies closer together, because of their refusal to acknowledge formally the postwar division of Europe. In this sense, Willy Brandt's "new" *Ostpolitik* and *Deutschlandpolitik* were policies of resignation, realizing that West Germany had to accept what existed in order to strengthen Bonn's position vis-à-vis the East. The *Ostpolitik* of the SPD and its coalition partner the Free Democratic Party (FDP) represented a West German acceptance of the postwar status quo, thus meeting Soviet and East German demands.

THE NEW OSTPOLITIK—GREAT EXPECTATIONS?

In an era in which there has been considerable disillusionment with the results of German *Ostpolitik* and *Deutschlandpolitik*, it is instructive to go back and remind oneself that, despite the atmosphere of success and at times euphoria within the SPD and FDP surrounding the completion of the various Eastern treaties, many of the major players were perhaps more realistic in their expectations than has subsequently been portrayed. Probably the most optimistic approach was that of SPD politician Egon Bahr, whose theory of *Wandel durch Annäherung* (change through rapprochement) argued that, by accepting the geographical status quo in Europe, including the existence of the GDR, the Federal Republic would ultimately be able to change the political status quo, and that a dialogue with the GDR would improve relations and lead to greater liberalization in East Germany, eventually permitting closer intra-German ties. Bahr's view could be termed the maximalist policy of those in the SPD leadership.

Brandt's position was somewhat less optimistic. His *Ostpolitik* was primarily defensive, "to maintain the substance of the nation," that is, the common ties that existed between the two Germanies. He expected that, by negotiating with the GDR without making German reunification a prior condition for any intra-German agreement, he would enable the Federal Republic to improve its contacts both with the GDR and the U.S.S.R. Brandt was prepared to recognize the concept of "two states in one nation," that is, West Germany gave *de facto* recognition to the GDR in the 1972 Basic Treaty, but refused to accord it full *de jure* recognition in international law. Because of this, the Chancellery and the Ministry for Intra-German Affairs, and not the Foreign Ministry, handle intra-German relations, trade with the GDR is not treated as foreign trade, and all East German citizens are eligible automatically for West German citizenship. In his memoirs, Brandt stresses that he did not expect the intra-German rapprochement to lead to reunification:

> I was well aware that, throughout its phases of historical development, Germany had never entirely corresponded to the 'classic nation state.' I nevertheless remained convinced that the nation would live on, even under differing political systems, because nationhood is a matter of awareness and resolve—Germany had always existed as a 'cultural nation, and it was as a 'cultural nation' that it would retain its identity.[1]

Although it is always difficult even with hindsight to determine exactly what politicians anticipate from their actions (if indeed they have clearly-defined expectations), one can say that Brandt's optimal expectation was a growing rapprochement between the two Germanies and the stress on Germany as a "cultural nation." However, the Federal Republic's *Deutschlandpolitik* was inextricably linked to its general *Ostpolitik*, including treaties with the U.S.S.R., Poland and Czechoslovakia. Taken together, there was more optimism about the overall implications of the new East-West policy than perhaps the individual intra-German negotiations warranted.

Moreover, the normalization of relations with East Germany was a prerequisite for enlarging West Germany's participation in international affairs, including membership in the United Nations. For instance, if it had not been for West German insistence, the 1975 Final Act of Helsinki would not have included the clause leaving open the possibility of German reunification, through the formula of "peaceful change" of boundaries.

One cannot discuss expectations, of course, without including the CDU/CSU. Throughout the three years of negotiations, the CDU and, even more so, the CSU, remained bitterly opposed to Brandt's *Ostpolitik* and *Deutschlandpolitik*, arguing that he had given away too much and received far too little in return. In particular, by recognizing the GDR, albeit only de facto, he had further diminished the possibility of reunification, without demanding a quid pro quo that gave the East Germans more freedom. Rainer Barzel, then Opposition leader and now president of the *Bundestag*, tried to topple the SPD-FDP coalition, and nearly succeeded. But the FDP and a few CDU members ensured that Brandt prevailed. In arguing against the treaties, however, the CDU did not put forward an alternative program. One could, therefore, say that the CDU-CSU in 1972 had no expectations, other than negative predictions, for the intra-German dialogue.

THE NEW OSTPOLITIK—GREAT DISAPPOINTMENTS?

In the past ten years, all parts of the German political spectrum (except for those on the extreme fringes) have come to agree that the intra-German rapprochement has brought some valuable concrete gains, but that these successes have been diminished by the GDR's policy of *Abgrenzung* (which is inadequately translated as "demarcation"). This policy has set distinct limits on the relationship and after the onset of the Polish crisis in 1980, led to a distinct deterioration in relations. Moreover, the decline in U.S.-Soviet relations is perceived in both German states to have detrimentally affected intra-German ties. The relationship between the two Germanies has indeed been a bellwether of East-West relations.

The greatest success of the intra-German rapprochement has been an increase in contacts between citizens of the two Germanies. These gains might not seem particularly important to an American thinking in global or geostrategic terms, but they have enormously improved the quality of ties between individuals in the two Germanies and are significant for the Germans. The improvements range from the ability to telephone between the two Germanies (and the two Berlins) without undue difficulty, to the substantial increase in visits between the two countries, although far more West Germans and West Berliners can visit East Germany than vice versa. Before the new *Deutschlandpolitik*, about 2.5 million West Germans visited the GDR every year. In 1979, the figure was 8 million (to a country with a population of 17 million). These family visits are probably the main reason for the Federal Republic's pursuit of its *Deutschlandpolitik*, but they have been detrimentally affected by the Polish crisis and the SED's concern about instability in the GDR. In October 1980, GDR leader Erich Honecker, in a direct assault on the intra-German relationship, doubled the minimum currency exchange requirement for visitors from West to East Germany, thereby deliberately reducing the flow and cutting back contacts between people. In 1982, only 5.75 million West Germans and West Berliners visited the GDR. Yet, despite this downward trend, the Federal Republic remains committed to the pursuit of an intra-German dialogue for humanitarian reasons.

The Federal Republic, one might argue, has also had a considerable effect on the domestic political situation in the GDR through the pursuit of *Deutschlandpolitik*. Some observers have argued that the normalization of relations with West Germany has destabilized East German society. Every night, as much as 85% of the East German population watches West German television, and this nightly emigration in one's living room is hardly a stabilizing factor. In a country that lacks a strong sense of national identity, the increasing contacts between the two Germanies have served to erode the already fragile domestic legitimacy of the government. To the extent that the greater penetration of East German society by West Germany destabilizes the society, the Federal Republic must ultimately ask itself whether it is in the West's interest to promote instability in Eastern Europe, particularly East Germany. If such instability led to widespread unrest and possible Soviet intervention, this might reverse the progress of the intra-German dialogue. For Bonn, the promotion of greater liberalization within the

GDR involves a delicate balance between encouragement of diversity and realization of the limits of such a policy.

Another successful aspect of the intra-German rapprochement has been the development of intra-German trade. The primary reason for this trade from the West German point of view is political rather than economic. Bonn has been willing literally to buy a variety of political concessions from East Berlin, from transit and communication compromises to the purchase of exit permits for some East Germans who want to leave the GDR. The total amount of currency transfers is estimated to be about 2.5 billion DM annually.[2] Bonn treats intra-German trade as neither foreign nor domestic trade, and the GDR is a de facto member of the European Economic Community. The Federal Republic also has special laws governing intra-German economic relations, and some Western specialists have argued that the privileged intra-German trade contacts enable high technology to find its way to the GDR, in defiance of the regulations established by the allied export control Coordinating Committee (CoCom) in Paris. Evidence on these questions is contradictory, but it is indisputable that the GDR benefits from these economic relations. Last year, intra-German trade rose by 13%, and the GDR had a trade surplus with the Federal Republic as a result of its import restriction policy, a product of its desire to reduce its hard currency debt.

These undoubted gains in intra-German relations have increasingly been offset by the GDR's hardening stance toward West Germany, which was exacerbated by the Polish events. The most dramatic example of *Abgrenzung*, because it directly affected contacts between Germans in the West and East, was the doubling of the currency exchange requirement. However, the GDR has also raised other demands which have detrimentally affected intra-German ties. Shortly after the doubling of the exchange requirement, Honecker, in a major address to party workers at Gera, abruptly abrogated the implicit understanding in the Basic Treaty. He demanded that West Germany recognize East German citizenship and cease automatically granting West German citizenship to refugees from East Germany. This demand is unacceptable to Bonn, which maintains that all citizens of both Germanies possess the right to West German citizenship. Moreover, the GDR insists that the Federal Republic upgrade its envoy in East Berlin from a permanent representative to an ambassador, which would imply that West Germany recognizes the GDR as a foreign country. Bonn refuses to do this. The two Germanies are at loggerheads on where exactly the boundary between the two countries on the river Elbe should be, and finally the GDR demands that West Germany close the Central Documentation Center at Salzgitter, which documents political repression in the GDR.

These GDR demands center around essentially the same dispute—the question of the GDR's sovereignty. The Federal Republic has refused to recognize the GDR's full sovereignty on any of these issues, but has attempted to keep the dialogue open. For instance, after several postponements, Chancellor Schmidt visited the GDR in December 1981, and, although Polish martial law was declared while he was there, he remained to finish his talks with Honecker. But all the West German negotiations have not persuaded the GDR to ease the policy of *Abgrenzung*.

THE INTRA-GERMAN RELATIONSHIP UNDER THE CDU/CSU-FDP COALITION

The intra-German relationship has been characterized by both continuity and change since Helmut Kohl replaced Helmut Schmidt in October 1982, and particularly since the CDU/CSU victory in the March 1983 election. The new government stressed continuity with the policies of the previous government in its November declaration: "Continuity is the acknowledgement of the tradition of a democratic Germany. Continuity in *Deutschlandpolitik* means the acknowledgement in the preamble of the Basic Law [the West German constitution] which summons the entire German nation to achieve its unity in freedom."[3] The new Minister for Intra-German Affairs, Heinrich Windelen, although a consistent opponent of the SPD-FDP *Ostpolitik* treaties ten years ago, has pledged that the Federal Republic will continue to uphold the treaties. The new government has also said that it does not regard reunification as a realistic goal for the foreseeable future, but that the development of intra-German ties is an important part of the administration's policy.

Initially there was a distinct sharpening of West German rhetoric about the GDR, particularly by the CSU and its leader Franz-Josef Strauss. In March and April 1983, the deaths of three West German citizens in the GDR, two of whom died while being questioned by East German border guards, led to charges of "murder" from Strauss, and to the cancellation by Honecker of his planned 1983 visit to the Federal Republic. Yet shortly thereafter, Strauss himself was instrumental in arranging a government guarantee for DM 1 billion in bank loans to the GDR, and a few weeks after the arrangement was announced, the Bavarian leader met with Honecker during a private trip to East Germany. Shortly thereafter, the GDR waived the currency exchange requirement for children under 15. The two German governments have recently concluded an eight-year postal agreement that will make it easier for West Germans to telephone and mail packages to people in East Germany. It appears unlikely, therefore, that there will be a major substantive decline in intra-German relations. However, West German rhetoric could become more critical, and Bonn may be more insistent in pressing East Berlin for concessions.

Despite the sharper rhetoric, it is, however, unlikely that the substance of intra-German relations will change dramatically under the present government. The quest for improved contacts has become one of the cornerstones of German policy, which has considerable significance for the electorate. No German government will readily forfeit the human gains of its *Deutschlandpolitik*. Indeed the CDU and CSU talk more about the need for closer intra-German ties as a prerequisite for reunification than does the SPD. During his July 1983 visit to Moscow, Kohl explicitly discussed the division of Germany. There is also growing talk of the interests of both German states in arms control. Although West German spokesmen admit that separate arms control talks between the two German states are impossible at the present time, it is nonetheless conceivable that they might occur in a better climate of Soviet-American relations. At a minimum, the present German government will remain committed to improving ties with the GDR and seeking to dilute Honecker's *Abgrenzung* policy. It certainly does not believe that reunification is imminent. However, it will not renounce the effort at *Annäherung*, even in the absence of *Wandel*.

The quest for a reunified, neutralist Germany is not dead, however. It has been revived in the last few years. This time, it is not the SPD that proposes this solution, but rather a variety of groups on the left, including part of the Green Party and the Berlin "Alternatives." Since the March election, the SPD has gone through a major process of reassessing itself, and it has moved further to the left, rejecting the deployment of U.S. missiles, which it initially proposed. However, there are few signs that the SPD will reopen the question of German neutralization and reunification. Egon Bahr has admitted his disappointment with the results of *Deutschlandpolitik*, and, even though he remains a German nationalist, would not favor neutralization.[4] It is the Peace Movement itself, or parts of it, that has revived these old ideas.

The advocacy of a reunified, neutralized Germany, free of the superpowers, is a distinct minority view in West Germany. But today it unites nationalists of the left and right. For instance, last year a group of authors published the book *Die deutsche Einheit kommt bestimmt*,

(German Unity Will Definitely Come), which contains a number of essays by left- and right-wing authors, all advocating the same theme: that German unity must take precedence over the Federal Republic's integration into the West. Authors such as Peter Brandt write about "patriotic internationalism," or "left-wing patriotism," and depict a world in which both superpowers leave Germany and it is reunited, with Berlin as the peaceful capital.[5] Echoes of these views can be found in diverse publications, but they remain fringe voices at the moment. Most Germans do not expect reunification, even if they want it, and the postwar generation is divided over the importance of this issue. The prevailing consensus is that the Federal Republic must preserve its special relations with the GDR, and, as an official recently put it, "We have certain national interests and as a loyal ally expect the U.S. to support them."

THE UNITED STATES AND THE INTRA-GERMAN RELATIONSHIP

The U.S.-German relationship has certainly come a long way since Washington tried to push a reluctant Bonn into improving relations with the U.S.S.R. in the early 1960s, and Adenauer complained "I can't stand any more of this wretched talk of detente." Whatever the U.S.'s views on eventual reunification, Washington has to accept Bonn's interest in closer intra-German ties for the sake of alliance cooperation. However, this West German interest inevitably inclines the Federal Republic toward maintaining a dialogue with the Soviet Union. The German commitment to detente has increasingly caused difficulties for the U.S. since the invasion of Afghanistan. The unwillingness to comply with U.S. economic sanctions was partly a product of Bonn's considerable economic stake in trade with the U.S.S.R.; but it was also linked to the Schmidt government's belief that the economic and political aspects of detente are connected—a viewpoint shared by the current government. A boycott of the Olympic games was as far as Bonn would go in supporting U.S. sanctions against the U.S.S.R. Similarly, West Germany has not been willing to respond to the Polish crisis with economic sanctions.

One might argue that the very success of Bonn's *Ostpolitik* and *Deutschlandpolitik* have caused increasing problems with the U.S. The Federal Republic disagrees with the U.S. on both the ends and means of dealing with the U.S.S.R., because it has a special interest to protect. Not only does West Germany support U.S. military policy in Europe, but former Chancellor Schmidt's suggestions were a major factor in the 1979 Two-Track NATO decision to deploy U.S. intermediate-range nuclear missiles if arms control talks fail. Yet its continuing interest in intra-German ties limits its willingness to declare detente over. Moreover, Bonn is concerned that the cooling of U.S.-Soviet relations should not have too great an impact on intra-German ties. Despite Kohl's victory and the greater West German emphasis on close ties with Reagan's Washington, it is highly unlikely that the new German government will eschew an interest in *Deutschlandpolitik.* There will, therefore, be continuing disagreements with the U.S. over how to respond to Soviet actions and how to interpret the Soviet threat.

The outlook for the intra-German relationship depends to some extent on the fate of the Intermediate Nuclear Force negotiations. Once the U.S. begins to deploy Pershing and cruise missiles, it is possible that the U.S.S.R. will choose to punish West Germany by creating more problems in intra-German relations, either in terms of a renewed raising of minimum currency exchange requirements, harrassments on transit routes to Berlin or trouble in Berlin. Indeed, President Andropov warned as much during Kohl's visit to the U.S.S.R. So far, the U.S.S.R. has deliberately maintained Berlin as an "oasis of detente" since the invasion of Afghanistan, to remind the Germans of their continuing dependence on the U.S.S.R. for tolerable relations with the GDR. But this could well change, depending on Soviet priorities. If there were a serious deterioration in the intra-German relationship, the U.S. might well face even greater opposition to continuing deployment from parts of the West German population, which would in turn lead to greater pressure from the Kohl government for some arms control solution and U.S. concessions. However, it is improbable that Bonn will cease to support deployment even if the Soviets use intra-German ties as a lever. Moreover, both the U.S.S.R. and the GDR would suffer economically from any significant deterioration in intra-German political relations. The West German loan guarantee to East Germany surely served as a reminder of the benefits to the GDR of the intra-German relationship, even after the deployment of new U.S. and Soviet missiles on German territory.

If U.S.-Soviet relations warm up (which appears unlikely in the near future), then intra-German ties probably will improve. However, there are limits to the intra-German relationship that exist irrespective of the climate of U.S.-Soviet relations. The GDR (and Soviet) fear of the destabilizing effects of closer ties with the Federal Republic will mean that *Abgrenzung* will remain a permanent feature of the intra-German nexus, creating constant tensions. The GDR will always blame West German and U.S. policy for deteriorating intra-German ties, because this is convenient. However, even if U.S.-Soviet ties were restored to their 1972 high point, the GDR would always fear the consequences of penetration by West Germany.

In short, the Federal Republic will remain frustrated in its attempts to bring the two Germanies closer together because of the GDR's fear of destabilization. However, it will equally continue to strive for improvements in these relations. It is possible that, when the "successor generation" comes to power in West Germany, the priority placed on intra-German relations may decline. After all, this generation has few memories of a united Germany. But the idea of Germany as a "cultural nation" remains and appears to affect the political consciousness of parts of the young generation. It is an integral component of German political culture. Nevertheless, it is conceivable that, by the end of the century, the quest for intra-German rapprochement may abate. This does not necessarily mean that West Germany would have fewer problems with the U.S. over the East-West relationship, however. The tradition of dealing with Russia also remains a part of German political culture.

West Germany depends on the U.S. for its security and on the U.S.S.R. for continuing ties with East Germany. It is therefore inevitably split between *Westpolitik* and *Ostpolitik*. Until it is willing to recognize formally that there are two German states and that reunification is not an option, this split German personality will remain. So far, the conflict between the two policies has not caused the U.S. undue problems. But to the extent that it makes Germany less willing to follow U.S. policy toward the U.S.S.R. and thereby exacerbates isolationist sentiment in the U.S. Congress, it could create future pressures to withdraw U.S. troops from Western Europe. The unresolved German question will always be a source of potential disagreements between Washington and Bonn over policy toward the U.S.S.R. But these conflicts should remain manageable, as long as there are no significant changes in the domestic or foreign policy orientations of the United States or Germany. If there are, then the German question will present itself again, possibly in a new form.

NOTES

1. Willy Brandt, *People and Politics: The Years 1960–1975* (London: Collins, 1978), p. 397.
2. J. Bethkenhagen and H. Machowski, *East-West Commercial Relations and their Wider Significance*, paper prepared for Centre for European Studies Conference (Brussels, December 1982), p. 20.
3. Bundesministerium für innerdeutsche Beziehungen, *Zur Deutschlandpolitik der neuen Bundesregierung* (Bonn, November 15, 1982)
4. Egon Bahr, *Was wird aus den Deutschen?* (Hamburg, Rowohlt, 1982)
5. See Wolfgang Venhor, ed., *Die deutsche Einheit kommt bestimmt* (Bergisch Gladbach: Gustav Lübbe, 1982)

4

The New Generation in Germany: Protest and Postmaterialism

Stephen F. Szabo

THE WEST GERMAN SUCCESSOR GENERATION

The West German-American relationship is in transition. A new generation of leaders will soon be coming to power on both sides. This generational changing of the guard will be occurring throughout Western Europe but is likely to have the most profound impact in West Germany, both because of the Federal Republic's key role in Western security and because of the impact of historical change on German security perspectives.

Recent German history has been characterized by severe and dramatic discontinuities. The formative historical experiences of a German born in the prewar period and of a postwar West German could hardly be more different. A German born before World War II and living in the Federal Republic of the early 1980s would have lived through a period of historical contrasts seldom experienced by one generation. He or she would have come of age either during the turbulent Weimar Republic, the Third Reich, World War II or the brutal postwar period. A West German of pensionable age in 1980 would have experienced all of these discontinuities and deprivations. Others of the prewar generations would have been shaped by the war and its aftermath. All would have also lived in the most stable, prosperous, peaceful and democratic era of German history, that of the Federal Republic.

In contrast, postwar Germans (who made up over half of the population in 1982 and will comprise two thirds of it by the end of the decade) have come of age in a society in which affluence, democracy and peace have been the norm. They are a generation which, in the words of Willy Brandt, "feels less burdened by the past, which did not take part in founding the Alliance but inherited it." A West German under the age of 40 in 1980 would have no direct experience or memory of the Marshall Plan, the Berlin Blockade, the formation of NATO or the Soviet occupation of Eastern Europe. Those under the age of 30 would have little or no memory of the building of the Berlin Wall. Most of the postwar generation grew up under detente rather than Cold War, and matured in a period when the United States represented Vietnam and Watergate.

This sharp break in historical experience has led to a growing concern that the next generation of German leaders will be less supportive of NATO and ties to the United States. The center of the German debate on the successor generation issue concerns this "emotional deficit" in the German-American relationship, combined with a growing tendency among younger Germans to equate the U.S. and the U.S.S.R. in political and moral terms.

Many German observers argue that the American generations which were produced by the East Coast Establishment and which had an emotional attachment to Europe—the John J. McCloys, Lucius Clays and Henry Kissingers—are being replaced by new American generations whose roots are in the Sunbelt and who are less informed or concerned about Europe. A similar process, it is argued, is occurring in the Federal Republic. Hans Ruehl, a leading German political scientist, argues in an article in *Die Welt* (April 22, 1980) that "the transatlantic estrangement has already begun" on both sides of the ocean:

> On the German side the ranks of those politicians become thinner who have experienced with awareness the United States as the liberator from a terrible dictatorship, as a generous helper in material misery and as a loyal friend in the days of danger for the young democracy, and who on their part have developed emotional links with the United States. They are being replaced by a generation of people who are in their fifties, who have studied or worked in the United States and who are united with the New World with many ties. But after them the prospects become dim.

A closer look at generational change in postwar West Germany will illustrate how German attitudes and values are changing and will permit some understanding of how these changes are influencing German images of the United States.

POSTWAR GERMAN GENERATIONS

In analyzing the postwar German experience, three generations emerge: the Skeptical Generation of the 1950s, the Protest Generation of the 1960s and the Post-Oil Shock Generation of the 1970s and early 1980s.

THE SKEPTICAL GENERATION

West Germans born in the period 1935—45 form what the sociologist Helmut Schelsky has named the "skeptical generation." It was a generation which matured during the period of reconstruction and the *Wirtschaftswunder* and was shaped by anticommunism and an environment of rapid economic growth. It was a "materialist" group in that it placed great emphasis upon economic achievements and security. Skeptical of ideologies and political involvement, it escaped into the small world of the secure, private existence. A politically conservative generation, it favored Adenauer and the Christian Democrats. Germans who matured during this difficult period developed a positive, idealized image of America, an image fostered by the exclusively Western orientation of the Adenauer years.

The American image in Germany underwent a remarkable change in the postwar period. Prior to World War II, America was of only peripheral interest to Germans. A dramatic change occurred after 1945. Germany emerged from the war shattered both physically and psychologically. A series of studies and surveys from the early 1950s found that America had become, as Günter Grass described it, an *Ersatzvaterland*. The attraction of American society was especially strong among young people.

Popular images of Soviet society, on the other hand, were overwhelmingly negative. Americans were described by the Germans as "progressive," "generous," and "practical" and there was a clear preference for both the democratic liberties and the standard of living of American society. The Soviets, in contrast, were characterized in these surveys as "hardworking" but "cruel," "domineering," and "backward." The Soviet image hit its low point following its suppression of the Hungarians in 1956, but even by 1963 responses to the U.S.S.R. elicited evaluations similar to those recorded in October 1954.

The surge in admiration for American society and things American was partly the result of a lack of alternative models. Not only was the Soviet model rejected but there was little interest in or admiration for the British or the French. As William Pfaff has observed, "Having abdicated politics, and even cultural autonomy, in the immediate postwar years, when nearly everything German seemed discredited, West Germany willed its dependence upon the United States." In many respects this admiration was rooted in the unusual circumstances of the postwar period and was sure to change as American predominance diminished and German self-confidence revived.

THE STUDENT PROTEST GENERATION

The first clearly postwar generation was that which was born between 1945 and 1959. It was the generation which matured during a period of affluence and expansion of higher education. In 1960, some 210,000 students attended universities; by 1970 the figure had grown to 420,000 and by the late 1970s over 900,000 students were enrolled. This massive influx into the universities produced the student protest movement known as the APO, or Extraparliamentary Opposition.

Centered in the universities, the APO was a reflection of the major expansion in university enrollments which began in the early 1960s and the impatience of students with the antiquated and authoritarian aspects of the university system. While the APO was primarily a protest against West German society and values, anti-Americanism was an important theme. The political shock of the Vietnam War was profound and resulted in a rapid and deep disillusionment with the United States. Two German writers described this generation's political engagement and contempt as "directed not only against the American world power, but against their own parents, almost all of whom were silent as they were during the Nazi barbarism." The idealized picture of America developed in the 1950s in Germany was shattered. The "outpost of the free West" became an imperialist power which used anticommunism as its justification. The "authoritarianism" and "fascism" of "Amerika" became associated with what was perceived by APO activists to be an oppositionless democracy of the CDU-SPD Grand Coalition government of 1966–69. The APO became not only an extraparliamentary opposition but an antiparliamentary movement as well.

While only a minority of university students were actively involved in the APO, tens of thousands marched against the Vietnam War and the Shah of Iran's visit to West Berlin. While many, perhaps a majority, of the university students of this 60s generation did not share the protest movement's views, the unquestioned acceptance of the American model was gone.

The APO reached its peak in the 1967–69 period and then dissolved into numerous splinter groupings. A few activists went into radical political "K-groups" (communist groups) or into the terrorist cells associated with the label of Baader-Meinhof. But the most significant political home for many APO activists became the Young Socialists (Jusos), the Social Democratic Party's youth organization.

The coming into power of the Social-Liberal coalition government of Willy Brandt and Walter Scheel in 1969 excited great expectations among the student left. Brandt represented a break with the past, not only from the *CDU-Staat* but from the Nazi past as well. He promised to create more democracy in West Germany, to open up the society and to redirect German foreign policy away from the anticommunist emphasis of Adenauer and in the direction of detente (*Ostpolitik*). The Brandt-led SPD won the votes of the majority of the generation of the 1960s and maintained its lead with this group into 1980.

The influx of APO activists into the Young Socialists was dramatic. The SPD registered a net gain in its membership of 222,048 during the 1969—72 period, with the most pronounced increases coming in the youngest age cohort. This influx was reflected also in a changing occupational structure within the SPD. Workers were being displaced by white-collar employees, students and civil servants. Obviously not all the new young members were active in the APO, but a substantial portion was, and it was this group which became active within the SPD youth organization.

The December 1969 national conference of the Young Socialists marked a turning point when it elected a member of this new group, Karsten Voigt, as its chairman and adopted a number of resolutions which attacked the centrist-moderate orientation of the SPD.

The main thrust of the Jusos was domestic. The primary concern of these activists was to renew the socialist orientation of the SPD and to overcome capitalism, thus creating "real" democracy at all levels of German society. American policy in Vietnam, however, was an important area of concern. A resolution of the 1969 Young Socialist Congress, for example, stated:

> The recently revealed massacre by U.S. troops in My-Lai, Vietnam has once again made clear to world public opinion the brutality of the U.S. military leadership in Vietnam. It is once more clear that the official goal, the defense of democracy in Southeast Asia, is simply a pretext for an imperialistic war which will lead to the extermination of the larger part of the Vietnamese people.

The Young Socialists increasingly equated the two superpowers as imperialist and urged a policy of detente with the East as a means of loosening the blocs and relaxing tensions.

The Jusos influence within the party waned after the replacement of Brandt with Helmut Schmidt in the Chancellery in 1974. The size of its active membership in 1977 was about half that of the 1972 total. The SPD had less appeal for a new generation of young Germans who were less interested in the large ideological movements of the 60s and were increasingly disenchanted with the major political parties. The Young Socialists, however, had a longer term impact in shaping the political values of a new generation of leaders within the SPD.

THE POST-OIL SHOCK GENERATION

Young Germans who were born after 1959 have matured in an affluent but increasingly insecure society. They are the products of the *Wirtschaftswunder* baby boom which peaked in the 1957—67 period. Consequently as America's population is becoming increasingly middle-aged, the Germans are experiencing a youth wave which is flooding schools, universities and the job market. These younger Germans, raised on high expectations, have become increasingly disappointed by both the economic slowdown and the deterioration of East-West relations. A recent poll found that only one in five of those under 25 years of age believes that the young will live better than their parents. Insecurity over job prospects has risen as youth unemployment has increased and the job prospects for university graduates have faded. Insecurity among the young has fostered a growing disillusionment with technology, technological progress and "the system."

The better educated portion of the postwar generations has experienced a significant change in values and expectations. Surveys have indicated clear trends toward a preference for "postmaterialist" values among these groups. Of the 10% in a 1977 survey who had an *Abitur* (the secondary school diploma) or university education, 37% were "postmaterialist" as compared to 14% who were "materialist." Postmaterialists stress quality of life issues over economic growth, civil liberties over order, participation in decision making over hierarchy, direct over indirect democracy and decentralized over centralized decision making styles. Value change is clearly associated with socialization in a relatively affluent society and a relatively stable international environment characterized by detente.

Postmaterialism has combined with economic and international insecurity to produce a critical attitude toward industrialism and modernism. This trend is part of a traditional current in German intellectual history with deep roots in German romanticism. In place of Spengler, however, young Germans have made bestsellers of *The Limits to Growth* and *Global 2000*.

Disillusionment has not been limited to technology but has made itself felt in the political arena as well. The young Germans of the post-oil shock generation have become disenchanted with the major political parties and other established political institutions. Many feel the parties to be unresponsive to the needs and interests of the average citizen. A number of recent scandals involving the major parties, trade union leaders and business executives have reinforced this image. The major parties are also seen by many of the critical young as supporting the suppression of civil liberties through the antisubversive laws of the 1970s and the critical stance of the parties toward demonstrations.

For this generation the Greens, the Peace Movement and the Citizen Initiatives (decentralized single-issue groups) as well as the Alternatives have become the forms of political expression. A 1981 survey conducted by Deutscher Shell, for example, found that of those between 15 and 24 years of age, 32% had no party affiliation, and 20% supported the Greens; 24% supported the SPD; 18% the CDU and 6% the FDP. Thus a majority did not support any of the major parties. In addition over 2 million Germans have joined Citizen Initiatives, and hundreds of thousands of the young have been active in the Peace Movement.

The Greens have replaced the Young Socialists as the major political expression of the 1970s generation. A decentralized structure, the original definition of itself as a movement rather than a party and its critique of the *Atomstaat* with its centralization and technocratic values, have all found a resonance with the younger audience. Its original anti-nuclear power and ecological thrust has broadened since 1981 to include anti-nuclear weapons positions as well. The result has been the formation of a diverse ECOPAX movement encompassing a wide variety of countercultural protest groups.

While the Peace Movement which appeared in 1981 was not solely a generational movement and a number of its leaders such as Erhard Eppler and Pastor Albertz were of the prewar generation, the vast majority of active participants in the movement are of the two postwar generations. Furthermore, surveys indicate that postwar Germans are more supportive of antiwar and antidefense attitudes than prewar Germans.

An analysis of a variety of surveys and studies of the basis of support for the peace movement indicate the following factors to be the most important in defining the profile of potential activists:

1. Under 36 years of age
2. High level of education
3. No strong attachment to the CDU or CSU
4. "Postmaterialist" value preference
5. Tendency toward unconventional political action (demonstrations, Citizen Initiatives, etc.)
6. Protestant or secular orientation

Age is the key variable which links these factors. Postwar Germans have more education than prewar Germans, they tend to prefer the SPD or the Greens to the Christian Democrats, they are more likely to have "postmaterialistic" values, to be involved in unconventional political action and to be less religious than prewar Germans.

The combination of this distinctive sociological background with a historical experience which stands in dramatic contrast to that of prewar Germans justifies the use of generational explanations in accounting for shifting values and perceptions.

GENERATIONAL CHANGE, VALUE CHANGE AND IMAGES OF AMERICA

Value change and generational change are having an important impact in altering perceptions of American society and policy. While surveys indicate that the majority of the German public opposes neutralism and continues to support the German link to the U.S. and NATO, young, better educated Germans are substantially more neutralist than their older counterparts. Numerous surveys and studies have found that those most critical of American society and American policies are the better educated and politically active young. Postmaterialists have a less positive view of the U.S. than those with more traditional values. While these groups are minorities, they are active and articulate and are likely to have a disproportionate impact on the future debate over German-American relations.

While these trends in value change can be seen in other advanced industrial states, their impact is especially profound in Germany because they intermesh with a long cultural tradition. A major theme of German intellectual history has concerned the issue of cultural affiliation with the West. The old tendency to contrast German culture and Western civilization has re-emerged once again in the questioning by many of the young of the dominant values of German society. The "Americanization" of West Germany represents a Westernization of German life, with the result that West Germany is a completely

Western country for the first time in German history. Cultures, however, are not as rapidly transformed as outward appearances might suggest, and the resurgence of a *Kulturkritik*, or cultural dissatisfaction, among the younger generation is evidence of at least a partial revival of traditional German cultural themes—that longing for communal values and the "inner life" which was characteristic of German romantics in the nineteenth and early twentieth centuries.

It is this "return of the repressed," as German political scientist Richard Löwenthal has termed it, which has given such intensity to the antinuclear, squatter and Alternative movements in the Federal Republic. The activists in the Green movement are both part of a postmaterialist activism within Western societies and the product of a longer cultural tradition. The growing critique of America may be part of this larger cultural critique of the West and its influence on Germany. For example, fully 81% of Green respondents in a 1981 survey viewed the United States as a "consumption and waste society which presents a horrible example for the rest of the world." In comparison, 60% of the national sample agreed with this view, which is an indication of the persistence of this traditional German attitude about American materialism.

Another important component of the critique of America concerns the attempt of a portion of the postwar generation to come to terms with the past. The legacy of the Third Reich was most intense for Germans who came of age in the 1960s. The APO was an assault upon an older generation which had either tolerated or supported Hitler and upon an America engaged in Vietnam. Many during the APO era believed Vietnam to be morally equivalent to Hitler's atrocities. Reinhard Lettau's pamphlet, *US=Täglicher Faschismus* and Ernest Nolte's comparison of Vietnam with Auschwitz were, as the historian Hans Gatzke has written, examples of attempts which "were motivated unconsciously by the hope of mitigating Germany's own past crimes." By bringing America down to the level of Nazi Germany, many Germans could relieve some of their guilt. If America, the teacher and model for postwar Germany, was capable of barbarism, perhaps the crimes of Hitler were not as uniquely German as some argued.

The tendency to equate the U.S. with Nazi Germany has grown to include the Soviet Union. References to the "two superpowers," Günter Grass' argument that after Vietnam America lost its moral authority, and Erhard Eppler's view that the Soviet invasion of Afghanistan was not qualitatively different from the American role in Vietnam are all examples of a disillusionment with an idealized America and an attempt to deal with the heavy burden of the past. The generation which came of age in the 1970s may not be as deeply concerned about the Hitler period and the issue of guilt. They, however, have known the United States only as an "ordinary country."

In summary, the U.S. image among the general public in West Germany has lost some of its luster but remains positive. The view of the U.S.S.R. remains overwhelmingly negative. These propositions hold for postwar Germans as well. However, an activist and articulate minority of the young, especially among the university-educated, hold either a skeptical or critical view of American society. Given the confluence of longstanding themes in German cultural development, the general trends in value change associated with advanced industrial societies, and the unique problems of dealing with a discredited past and of shaping a new identity—all of which have been experienced and perceived most intensely by postwar German intellectual elites and their student audiences—it appears predictable that criticism and skepticism about American society will grow in West Germany. The postwar generations do not have the emotional link to the U.S., that unique combination of subservience and awe shaped by the immediate postwar years, that dominated the 1950s.

IMPLICATIONS FOR GERMAN-AMERICAN RELATIONS

Given the dramatic discontinuities of recent German history, the rapid pace of economic and social change, the transformation of the international environment and the sheer size of the postwar German generation, it would be rather surprising if substantial generational change did not occur. The greater readiness to challenge established authority, legacies of the "undigested past," as well as the age-old issue of identity which has preoccupied all German generations constitute a volatile mix. The questioning of values and of the relationship to the United States is part of a normalization process associated with the recovery of the nation.

While it is unrealistic to expect that younger Germans would inherit the views of a previous generation shaped in a different historical context, a danger exists that an overreaction will occur in which an idealized America is replaced by an America which is an antimodel. Blaming the U.S. for their insecurity and overcompensating for dependence by rejecting future cooperation, the new generation of Germans could push the Federal Republic down a path toward a destabilization of both German and European security.

It is crucial, therefore, that contacts between the new generations of Germans and Americans be established and intensified. Both governmental and private organizations must increase their efforts to bring the emerging new leaders from both countries together. Increased contacts may not result in agreement on all issues, but they should foster an appreciation of the diversity of viewpoints that characterizes both societies and, most importantly, an appreciation of the openness of Western political systems. At the least, exchanges may temper the tendency of many young Germans to think of the U.S. and the Soviet Union as "the two superpowers" or to think of the Americans as being somehow apart from the Western political and cultural tradition. Finally they should provide a richer context for understanding the interests and points of view of the other side.

The American view of the relationship also must be altered. The American public's views of West Germany tend to be based upon stereotypes about Germans which are either dated or exaggerated. Most Americans receive their image of West Germany from television or the press, and reporting tends to emphasize such sensational aspects of German life as Neo-Nazism, terrorism and demonstrations. A viewer of American television could easily conclude that the history of Germany ended in 1945, since the majority of television treatment of German affairs centers on Hitler and the Holocaust. While the importance of teaching the lessons of this epoch is indisputable, the problem of balance also arises. Too few Americans have developed an image of the new Germany, and many are quick to adopt the worst interpretations of German motives.

The German-American relationship is clearly in a period of transition. Americans will have to learn to live with a more independent and assertive West Germany. Younger Germans in turn will have to develop a mature and realistic image of America. Both societies will have to view the other as normal rather than in either idealized or threatening ways.

5

The 1983 National Elections: Three Winners and a Loser

Robert Gerald Livingston

As they have nine times since World War II, voters in the Federal Republic turned out in great numbers March 6, 1983, to elect the 498 members of their national parliament, the *Bundestag*. Over 89 percent of the 44 million eligible cast their ballots—an impressive participation rate, which puts the United States to shame, with its 50–54 percent in presidential elections. As with every election, the voters did not so much initiate change as confirm a change of government which the powerful political parties had previously arranged among themselves. In this election they gave their approval to formation of a coalition between the Christian Democrats (CDU/CSU), led by Chancellor Helmut Kohl, and the Liberals, the FDP. The new coalition had already taken over on October 1, 1982, when the FDP deserted the Social Democrats (SPD), the partner with which it had governed the country for the previous thirteen years, and allied itself with the Christian Democrats.

If in one sense the March 6 elections served as the electorate's confirmation of an earlier shift of forces within the parliament, they also represented much more than that. They reflect the contours of a party political landscape that will in some ways be more like that of the 1950s than that of the 60s or 70s and in other ways decidedly different.

Three parties won, the Christian Democrats handily, the Liberals narrowly, and a new party, the Greens, surprisingly. The SPD suffered severe losses. (See table on page 46.)

THE 1983 NATIONAL ELECTIONS

An analysis of these elections, of the issues that determined their outcome, and of the directions which they suggest for future German politics requires first an understanding of an electoral system which combines features of proportional and plurality systems, and of the political parties which have come over the past two decades to dominate what is often called a *Parteienstaat* (party state) in Germany.

MODIFIED PROPORTIONAL REPRESENTATION

German voters cast two ballots, a "first vote" for the candidate in the voter's home district and a second for a party list. Notwithstanding an extensive public education campaign over many years, not all German voters understand the political difference between these two votes. It is crucial, however. The second vote, for the party list, determines the *total* number of *Bundestag* seats a party will receive. Seats won by the first, the vote for its individual candidates, are subtracted from a party's total. The more district seats a party wins, the fewer party-list seats need be added to make up its total. Let us say that a party wins 50 percent of the second, the party-list votes (in practice only once has a party won as much as 50 percent, the CDU/CSU in 1957). That party is assigned 248 *Bundestag* seats, 50 percent of the total.

From those 248 are then deducted all the "direct mandates," those seats won directly by the big names such as the SPD's Helmut Schmidt or by local "matadors" with strong backing at the grass roots. The party lists for which voters cast their second ballot are set up by the party organizations in the individual eleven *Länder* (states)—one explanation of the enormous power which the parties wield in politics. Prominent personalities and representatives of key interest groups— farmers and businessmen in the case of the CDU/CSU, for instance, or trade unionists in the case of the SPD—are placed sufficiently high on the lists to ensure them a *Bundestag* seat, even if they should lose in their district. Such losses are considered quite normal and do not lessen the loser's authority nationally or in parliament. Leaders such as Chancellor Kohl, who is chairman of the CDU, or Hans-Dietrich Genscher, his counterpart in the FDP, regularly fail to carry their districts. They enter the parliament because they are "secured" by being placed high up on the *Land* list.

On March 6, the CDU/CSU's 48.8 percent entitled it to 244 seats—just five short of an absolute majority. Its direct candidates scored well, winning 180 first-vote seats. Sixty-four party-list seats were then added to make up its total of 244. In the case of the SPD, which garnered 38 percent of the vote entitling it to 193 seats, only 68 candidates, almost half of them in the party's bastion of North Rhine-Westphalia, got enough first votes to win. The SPD was accordingly assigned 125 list seats. Neither the FDP nor the Greens could win a single direct seat. All their 34 and 27 *Bundestag* members respectively came from their lists.

Party-list voting is modified in a decisive way: to gain any seats at all a party must win at least five percent of the national vote. The Federal Republic's founding fathers and their advisers from the occupying powers wished to prevent a proliferation of parties, a development which, they believed, had fatally weakened the Weimar Republic before World War II. They achieved, perhaps overachieved, their aim. The number of successful parties declined steadily during the 1950s. Between 1961 and 1982 only three found their way into the *Bundestag*: CDU/CSU, FDP, and SPD.

A final feature of the electoral system, also unanticipated and undesired by the founding fathers, should be noted. Since 1953, national elections have been increasingly won and lost not by the parties but by those men whom they designate as their "chancellor candidates." Ever since the great CDU leader of the 1950s, Konrad Adenauer, built up a party around him the voters have known in voting for one of the two major parties whom they were selecting to head the government. *Kanzlerdemokratie* has flourished because a series of strong and talented chancellors, notably Adenauer, Brandt and Schmidt, recognized, exploited and extended the constitutional powers of the office. Voters last March again felt they were deciding between combinations, Helmut Kohl within the context of his party and Hans-Jochen Vogel within the context of his. There is little doubt that they chose the stronger, more united combination.

The electoral system, the hybrid, personalized proportional representation, the power of the parties, and the focus upon the chancellor candidates have assuredly given the electorate what Germans of the 1940s sought so desperately after the turmoil, vicissitudes and collapse of the 1918–1945 period: stability and continuity. There have been but two genuine changes of government since the first *Bundestag* elections in 1949. The CDU/CSU led the governments for twenty years, first under Adenauer and then under Ludwig Erhard and Kurt-Georg Kiesinger; the SPD led them for thirteen years under Brandt and Schmidt. Even ministers were seldom changed during these extended periods. Compared to the highly volatile and responsive U.S. electoral system, the German system changes very slowly. Germans like it that way. The price of this stability, of course, is an unresponsiveness to altered public attitudes and failure to address new issues. This sluggishness helps explain the Greens' success last March.

The 1983 elections may best be analyzed by examining them from the viewpoint of those essential elements of the German political system, the political parties, which are constitutionally recognized as vehicles of political expression. The two big established parties, the CDU/CSU and SPD—and even the small FDP and Greens in a certain sense, too—are catchall organizations. While all have core constituencies, all also frame their programs and campaigns to appeal to the widest possible spectrum of social and occupational groups. All four except the Greens—and that may yet come—have developed bureaucratic machines which inform and propagandize voters and conduct lavish campaigns with support from the state. All receive from the public treasury DM 3.5 for each vote, free television spots, and other less overt subsidies as well.

The following table compares the 1983 with the 1980 election results.

THE RESULTS OF THE 1980 AND 1983 ELECTIONS

Party	1983		1980		Plus/Minus	
	Percent	Seats	Percent	Seats	Percent	Seats
CDU/CSU	48.8%	244	44.5%	226	+4.3%	+18
SPD	38.2	193	42.9	218	−4.7	−25
FDP	7.0	34	10.6	53	−3.6	−19
Greens	5.6	27	1.5	—	+4.1	+27
Others	0.4	—	0.5	—	−0.1	—

Notes to Table

Berlin, which remains under special occupation status, sends 22 appointed members to the *Bundestag* but they do not vote on substantive matters.

The 498 seats in the 1983 *Bundestag* consist of 248 direct mandates and 250 party-list seats (including two "surplus" seats that resulted from vote-counting technicalities).

Source: Bulletin, Presse- und Informationsamt der Bundesregierung, Nr. 29/1983, S. 251.

CDU/CSU—TRIUMPH AND RESTORATION

Helmut Kohl led the CDU and Franz Josef Strauss the CSU to a smashing victory. Their combined 48.8 percent was the best result for the CDU/CSU since 1957, with the parties collecting the largest number of votes (19 million) ever. Except in the Saarland, the CDU registered gains of four percent or better in all *Länder*. The CDU/CSU emerged as the strongest party in nine of the eleven states, leaving the SPD with majorities in only two, the city-states of Hamburg and Bremen. Its 11-point lead over the Social Democrats country-wide was its largest in twenty-five years.

Had first votes alone counted, those for the CDU/CSU's individual candidates, the triumph would have been enormous. Over 52 percent of the first votes went to the CDU/CSU, well over 20 million of them. But it gained only 19 million second votes. How did the missing million CDU/CSU voters cast their second ballots? Most gave them to the FDP lists. So strong in effect was the CDU/CSU surge that it carried not only its own candidates into the *Bundestag* but the FDP list candidates as well.

The Christian Democrats made deep inroads into the SPD's core constituency, the working class, particularly in the smaller cities of Baden-Württemberg in the South, where factories had been laying off large numbers, but also in the big "smokestack" cities of the Rhine-Ruhr region—Essen, Dortmund, Mühlheim and the like. For the first time in eighteen years, the party emerged stronger than the Social Democrats in the industrial heartland, the state of North Rhine-Westphalia. One of the givens of Germany's political geography has been the dominance of the CDU/CSU in the predominantly Catholic parts of the country, mainly the South and Southwest, and of the SPD in the predominantly Protestant ones, mainly the North. This time the Christian Democrats registered unusually strong gains in the North also, all but wiping out this differentiation.

A final feature of the CDU/CSU triumph worth considering was its strong first-vote performance: it won 180 of 248 direct *Bundestag* mandates at stake, all of them from its major opponent, the SPD. In the 1980 elections only 121 direct mandates had been won by the Christian Democrats. The shift of 59 between the two big parties—almost a quarter of all the direct mandates—is a striking measure of the extent of the CDU/CSU resurgence.

The seventies, particularly the period 1973–1977 when Kurt Biedenkopf was the CDU's general secretary (i.e., its professional manager) and the period 1980–83 following the defeat of the CSU's Franz Josef Strauss in the 1980 national elections, were the years of regeneration. It paid off in 1983 at the polls. Of course the CDU/CSU ł large and solid base upon which to rebuild after it was forced government in 1969. One sometimes forgets that the Christian L crats and their Bavarian allies have won pluralities or better in ni the ten national elections. They can count on a loyal core of 3ί percent of the electorate.

Their basic constituency consists of the middle class, fa professionals, self-employed and middle-level managers, ar *Beamten*, the civil servants at local, national and especially stat who constitute a strong, organized and generally conservative p force. The CDU/CSU is not—and this is too often forgotten in the States when the label "conservative" is attached to Kohl's p middle-class, a bourgeois party. It has always attracted good ε among the working class, particularly skilled workers everywhen Josef Strauss's notable achievement with the CSU has been to into what is a Bavarian populist party, with supporters in all cl in towns as well as the countryside. Within the CDU, the old left traditions of the prewar Catholic Center party live on within th called Social Committees (*Sozialausschüsse*), wryly dubbed "Sέ Heart of Jesus Socialists," who draw inspiration from the social ju encyclicals of Popes John XXIII and John Paul II.

In the Federal Republic, whose voters are about half Catl and half Protestant, religious issues have virtually disappeared national politics. The Roman Catholic hierarchy sometimes still tempted to intervene on behalf of the CDU/CSU, as it did three ɣ ago. This time around it refrained. The designation "Christian" is completely meaningless among the German electorate, however, those voters who tell pollsters that they are "church-going" or "pɪ ticing" Catholics and Protestants are far more likely to vote CDU/C than they are SPD. In a country where over 90 percent of the populat remain inscribed members of the two great and state-establish churches, the CDU/CSU retains an important advantage as the par which was deliberately established in 1947 as a political vehicle fc both Protestants and Catholics. To this day it takes exquisite car to balance party offices and candidates between members of tht two churches and to try to project a Christian image on appropri- ate occasions.

To a large degree, the CDU/CSU's victory was that of Helmut Kohl—at least to the clear extent that a CDU/CSU which already had all the prerequisites for victory in 1980 but had the wrong chancellor candidate, Franz Josef Strauss, was able to exploit these prerequisites in 1983 with the more appealing Kohl, a candidate of consensus rather than controversy, caution rather than impulse. Unlike the Strauss-Schmidt election in 1980 or that between Adenauer and Brandt in 1961, the 1983 election was not really a personality contest. Neither Kohl nor his Social Democratic opponent projected himself vividly on the hustings or in the media.

More important in accounting for the CDU/CSU's victory was its transformation during the last decade from a coalition of state and local organizations so loose as to belie the party's customary designation in German political jargon as "the Union" into a modernized, tightly organized, effective machine supported by a large membership. It may have overtaken the hierarchical and more traditionally organized SPD in efficiency. The party launched a membership drive after its humbling defeat in 1969. By 1980 it had restored its strength and had attained a membership of 800,000. With these assets the CDU/CSU may well have begun a new era of dominance, one that rests upon more solid organizational foundations than during its earlier period of preponderance, from 1949–1966.

THE SPD—DIVIDED AND DEFEATED

Unlike the CDU, which is barely 30 years old, the Social Democratic Party can look back on over a hundred years of history. It descends directly from the great socialist thinkers of the nineteenth and early twentieth centuries, Karl Marx, Friedrich Engels, Ferdinand Lassalle and August Bebel, from a parliamentary group that on the eve of World War I was the biggest in the Wilhelminian *Reichstag*, and from an organization that before Hitler extended throughout what is today West Germany, East Germany, and parts of Poland and the Soviet Union. Defeated often and usually in opposition during the *Reich* and the Weimar Republic, the SPD of 1983 may be taking some comfort in this history and the sense of certainty which it provides that the party will rise again.

The Social Democrats have always failed to better their Christian Democrat rivals nationally, except for the heady victory of 1972, when the voters, approving Willy Brandt's *Ostpolitik*, gave the SPD a tiny plurality. Unlike the CDU/CSU, it has never come anywhere near an absolute majority. In the early years of the Federal Republic, the SPD remained working-class oriented, largely pacifist, and imprisoned in a traditional Marxist intellectual framework. Throughout the 1950s it hovered around 35 percent. Only with the decisions of 1959 and 1960, with the adoption of the so-called Bad Godesberg program, did the party shed its working-class image, jettison most of its Marxist ideological baggage, and accept the rearmament of West Germany and its membership in the Western alliance. Then the party began to grow.

Two experienced, talented and popular chancellors, Brandt from 1969–1974 and Schmidt from 1974–1982, helped broaden the party's appeal sufficiently so that, in coalition with the Liberals, it was able to gain, hold, and at least in foreign policy wield power effectively throughout the 1970s. As early as 1975, the first signs of disarray and decline became evident. With Strauss as its candidate, the CDU/CSU was unable to exploit these openings in 1980. But in 1983 came the debacle.

The SPD was the single loser last March, skidding to 38.2 percent of the vote, its worst performance since 1961. Three main reasons account for the defeat. First, the party was simply played out, used up. In power for 16 years, first with the CDU/CSU in the Grand Coalition of the 1960s and then with the FDP, the SPD had drafted its best talents from municipal and *Land* governments, from the *Bundestag*, from the unions, and elsewhere for government posts in Bonn. Pragmatic compromises which wielding power requires had alienated many left-wingers in the party, to whom principles and ideology are unusually important. Strife and bickering emerged after 1977, and German voters characteristically have a low tolerance for personal quarrels in politics, as Arnulf Baring, a perceptive historian of the period, has observed.

The second and most immediate cause of defeat was the natural inclination of voters to hold the SPD responsible for the economic downturn and resultant unemployment, which rose to 10 percent during 1983, an unheard-of high. The Social Democrats had displayed skilled economic management in the late 1960s by the SPD's economics minister, Karl Schiller, at the time of the first oil price shock in 1973–74 by Schmidt as finance minister, and during the weakness of the U.S. dollar during 1977–79 by Schmidt as chancellor. However, they had not been able to deal as skillfully with the second oil price shock of 1978–79: inflation, always a bugaboo to Germans, climbed; the current account swung into deficit for the first time in many years; and government indebtedness rose sharply during 1980–82—all of which reawakened old prejudices and suspicions that the Social Democrats do not understand economics, cannot handle finances, and are spendthrifts.

Kohl's CDU/CSU exploited this weakness to the hilt. Its slogan, "Vote for Recovery," was well chosen. The voters showed that they preferred to try the CDU's remedies of a sharp curtailment in government spending and tax stimulation for investments instead of shopworn SPD deficit financing prescriptions.

A third, more subtle reason is to be found in the Social Democrats' indecisiveness, both on specific issues and in their overall approach to the electorate. The party's leadership was divided and it equivocated on the only foreign policy issue in the campaign, installation of new American medium-range missiles in the Federal Republic pursuant to an Atlantic alliance decision of 1979. Although Schmidt had fathered this NATO decision, much of his party was opposed to the missiles, mainly out of fear that their deployment would set back the good relations with the East—and particularly with the Soviet Union—which had been the result of the SPD's *Ostpolitik* of 1969 –74, the most significant achievement of Germany's postwar foreign policy. The Christian Democrats were successful in painting the SPD's indecisiveness as opposition to the Atlantic alliance itself and to the United States, both of which enjoy strong support among the voters.

Indecisiveness was also caused by acrimonious division within the party on which constituencies to attract. For one group, the first SPD priority was to hold on to traditional support among the workers, who fear unemployment, who count upon the general benefits of the German welfare state and the extensions of it during the period of SPD/FDP rule, and who also remain attached to old-fashioned national, familial, and social values, much like their blue-collar ethnic counterparts in the United States. On the other hand, an important element in the party leadership, one with which its chairman Willy Brandt identified, sought a "majority to the left of the CDU"—that is, by attracting the educated, middle-class young who reject traditional values in favor of the "postindustrial" concerns of environmentalism, feminism and pacifism. The aim of the strategy advocated by this second group was to woo voters away from the ecology/peace party, the Greens.

Unable to choose fully between these two constituencies and plagued by inept campaign management as well, the SPD ended up hemorrhaging votes in both directions—working-class voters to the CDU on the right and young, educated middle-class voters, the very people who had flocked to the party in its victorious years from 1966 –72, to the Greens on the left. Post-election estimates put the loss at 1.4 –1.6 million votes to the Christian Democrats and perhaps 250,000 to the Greens. (Had the party not gained 200 –300,000 from the Liberals, the results would have been little short of disaster.)

It is difficult to estimate precisely how great a contribution a switch in chancellor candidates made to the SPD's defeat. Not having Helmut Schmidt at the top again may have cost the party as many as a million votes. A popular mayor of Munich during the 1960s and a competent and liberal minister of housing and then of justice during the late 1970s, Hans-Jochen Vogel lacked Schmidt's charisma, authority and international experience. Voters doubted his ability to deal with the party's left wing, which had caused Schmidt endless trouble. Unsure in his control of the party, even though the traditionally disciplined SPD rallied faithfully around him as a standard-bearer during the campaign, Vogel tended to straddle on some important issues. Almost half of his own party members indicated in public opinion surveys that they would have preferred Schmidt as candidate again, although he had already declared his refusal to run early in the autumn of 1982.

An SPD with almost two-fifths of the vote need not despair. But it faces many serious problems resulting from societal and demographic trends. Its core remains the blue-collar workers, but as a percentage of the labor force these have dropped from over 50 percent three decades ago to less than 40 percent today, and this trend will continue as manufacturing is replaced by high-tech and service industries. Still most union-organized working men and women will doubtless stick with the SPD. "Practicing" unionists, surveys continue to show, are much more likely to vote Social Democratic than CDU, even though there is no formal tie between the unions and the SPD, as there is between the British unions and the Labour party.

The chief factors of SPD growth in the 1960s were its ability to attract the female vote and also the new middle class of white-collar employees and mid-level supervisors in organizations, firms and government—a constituency which made up only a bit more than 20 percent of the workforce in 1950 but constituted 46 percent by 1980. The SPD was notably successful in recruiting the sons and daughters of the middle-class teachers, officials, and Protestant clergy as members. Their loyalty grew tepid, though, during the 1970s and many deserted to the Greens last March. A particularly worrisome trend has been the SPD's recent weakness in major cities which in the fifties and sixties were its bastions. Cities like Berlin, Frankfurt, Stuttgart and Munich are now in the hands of popular CDU or CSU mayors.

In the cities and in *Länder* like Lower Saxony, Bavaria and Baden-Württemberg the SPD has to start rebuilding if it is to regenerate itself in opposition.

Many predict at least twelve years in the wilderness. Even Schmidt predicts eight. Judging by the slow pace of past political change in Germany, such estimates may not be far off the mark.

THE FDP—FORTUNATE BUT FADING

Why count the Liberals among the winners, when they dropped from 10.6 percent in 1980, their best result in almost twenty years, to seven percent last March? A month before the election, few observers would have given them any chance at all to surmount the five percent hurdle. Political analysts put their core, first-vote strength at only two to three percent. Their leaders Hans-Dietrich Genscher, the Foreign Minister, and Otto Count Lambsdorff, Minister of Economics, ranked at the bottom in popularity surveys among German voters. For the past several years the FDP has been losing support in all states. It is now represented in only four of the eleven *Landtage* (state legislatures).

Its election chances looked so bleak because Schmidt had skillfully maneuvered in September so that Genscher and his FDP became in the public mind chiefly to blame for the breakup of the coalition, thus earning a reputation for inconstancy and betrayal. The SPD's charges of faithlessness were not without validity, for the Liberals' good performance in 1980 had been owing in large part to their campaign assurances that voting for the FDP would make the SPD's Schmidt, the country's most popular political leader, chancellor once again. Hesitant and shifty tactics by Genscher, who all throughout 1982 gave clear signs that he was thinking of pulling out of Schmidt's coalition but could not quite bring himself to it, also helped dim the party's electoral image.

In March the FDP in fact gained less than three percent of the first vote, a sign that its core support had shriveled away. But to the astonishment of many analysts it captured seven percent of the second vote, enough to put it into the *Bundestag* again even though it came nowhere near winning a single direct seat. With less than 1.1 million first but over 2.7 million second votes, the FDP found 1.6 million voters who wanted them in the *Bundestag* enough to split their ballot. Most of these ballot-splitters came from the CDU.

Such deliberateness of choice is high testimony to the sophistication of the German electorate. Had the FDP not surmounted the five percent barrier, the CDU/CSU would have almost certainly gained more than the 249 seats required for a majority. That would have made Strauss vice-chancellor and probably foreign minister. National power for the CSU leader, who is widely distrusted and disliked outside his native Bavaria, as the 1980 election had shown, was just what voters did not want. They feared a man who had been quoted before the campaign as saying that "I don't care who serves as chancellor under me." It was largely to keep Strauss out of power that they cast enough second votes for the FDP to keep it in parliament.

THE 1983 NATIONAL ELECTIONS

The Liberals were thus unexpectedly given a fresh chance to play their traditional and influential role as the maker and breaker of coalitions in German politics. Every governmental change in Germany since the 1950s has resulted from an FDP decision to defect from either the CDU or the SPD. This fact has given the party enormous leverage, which tactically skilled leaders like Walter Scheel in the 1960s and Genscher today have exploited handsomely, making the party more powerful in the *Bundestag* than in the country and more powerful in the cabinet, where it has demanded and received important ministries such as Foreign Affairs or Economics, than in the parliament. As the Liberals proved again when they deserted Schmidt's government last autumn, they possess a vital sense of survival, ready to leave a sinking ship just before it goes to the bottom.

For all its survival skills, however, the big change has this time left the FDP so weakened that it may be spent as a force in German politics. The 1.6 million votes which the party "borrowed" this time and which put it into the *Bundestag* cannot even be called swing votes, for they came from calculating CDU supporters whose loyalties do not even temporarily lie with the Liberals. They cannot be counted upon by Genscher.

The Liberals have been the party of the small businessman, middle-level industrial management and well-to-do professionals. Losses may, observers joke, reduce it to a "triple A" club, the *Ärzte Advokaten-Apotheker* (doctors-lawyers-pharmacists) party. It has traditionally stood strongly for civil rights and for a free, competitive market economy of the kind that fueled Germany's economic boom of three decades ago. Chief of the free marketeers is Count Lambsdorff, the FDP economics minister, who took the lead in bringing down the SPD/FDP coalition last year with his demands for drastic cutbacks of the state's role in the economy. Advocates of civil rights, the other sturdy plank in FDP platforms, have lost strength. Several leaders among them resigned from the party, refusing to accompany it in deserting the Social Democrats. Tussles within the government during the summer of 1983 over legislation to control public demonstrations have given proof of FDP weakness on such issues.

In the past the FDP has always displayed uncanny regenerative powers because it has been able to fulfill voters' expectations that it would balance and constrain the bigger parties, checking the Social Democrats from slipping too far left or the Christian Democrats from moving too far right for the tastes of a centrist electorate. It is questionable whether the FDP is strong enough to play such a role under Kohl.

It cannot plausibly threaten to rejoin the Social Democrats, it lacks a broad basis in the *Länder*, and it has failed to develop an attractive younger generation of leaders. It seems doomed to a period of subservience to the CDU/CSU, which may rob it of the unique profile as a counterweight that has constituted its great appeal, and may cause it to fade away before this decade is over.

THE GREENS—OUTSIDERS AS INSIDERS

The Greens were winners simply because they succeeded in entering the *Bundestag*. With only 27 of the 498 seats, their parliamentary strength is not formidable. But their success is remarkable because it breaks a longstanding CDU/CSU-SPD-FDP oligopoly. Not since 1957 has a fourth party made it into the national parliament.

Their victory caps a rapid growth: in less than five years the Greens have won representation in six of the eleven state parliaments, displacing the Liberals in many of them. More than one thousand Green representatives now sit in communal, municipal and *Land* legislatures. The party also exercises an influence that is greater than its elected strength because it surfaces fresh, modern issues that the established parties have long neglected and left to outsiders such as the extreme left and, more recently, the Greens.

Like the FDP, the Greens succeeded because voters—in this case mostly SPD adherents—split their ballots, giving them their second vote. Their core is larger and, based as it is upon a subculture in German society, more cohesive than the FDP's. About 1.7 million voters gave the party their first vote, 600,000 more than the Liberals could capture.

The Greens are something new on the political scene: an issue-oriented amalgam of ecologists, antinuclearists, leftists, feminists and urban populists, one which seeks to remain partly outside the political mainstream, to function both as a party and as a movement. They are ready to violate established rules of the political game upon occasion. Their main focus has been upon environmental issues, with which the established parties failed to deal successfully during the 1970s. But increasingly since 1979 the Greens have seized upon the antinuclear and peace issues, attacking sharply NATO's decision to install new medium-range missiles, the Pershing II and cruise, in the Federal Republic. In their opposition to the missiles, the Greens are reflecting a concern that is widespread. Some polls show well over half the population to be against the Pershing and cruise deployments. The

Greens also endorse neutralism for Germany and withdrawal from the alliance—both issues where, however, they run counter to majority public opinion.

For all the emphasis upon environment, the Greens are a party of the cities. Their vote reached eight to nine percent in the city-states of Hamburg and Bremen and exceeded ten percent in university towns such as Freiburg and Tübingen in the Southwest, an early Green stronghold. Their core supporters are the highly educated graduates of universities or teachers' training schools, many of them disillusioned SPD voters. The Greens' strength is to be found among the 30 to 35 age group; middle-aged women; and those who provide educational, health, and social services—people who, as a Social Democrat quipped, are "reformers with a claim to a state pension" and who are oriented to postindustrial values and quality-of-life issues. The pool of potential Green supporters is growing as Germany develops into a service sector economy.

For many young voters the appeal of the Greens derives from widespread disenchantment with the *Parteienstaat*, the stifling monopoly of the three established parties which penetrates so many bureaucratic, educational and economic organizations in Germany. The Greens boast that they are an "antiparty party" in order to cater to this attitude. The party raises a broad challenge to traditional values of economic growth, personal achievement, and the work ethic. Of course the Greens themselves, as their opponents delight in pointing out, are a product of the affluent society and the economic growth that they despise, able to pursue "postindustrial" values because the hard work of their parents produced the resources to finance a lavish welfare state which supports them when they become sick or unemployed. The Greens are not, however, political drop-outs. They are rather an outgrowth of the citizen initiatives movement of the early 1970s, which was addressed to local political issues. In their effort to broaden political participation and citizen responsibility, the Greens are moving the Federal Republic another step along its transition from Prussian hierarchical to Western pluralistic forms of democracy.

The party's long-term prospects are uncertain. Having tied themselves so closely to the missile issue, they may lose momentum once it vanishes. Kohl has predicted that, riven by tensions, they will self-destruct. Certainly they are subject to many contradictory forces which are difficult to reconcile: between fundamentalists, such as their hyperactive spokesperson Petra Kelly, and pragmatists, such as the practiced Berlin lawyer Otto Schily; between their parliamentary and extraparliamentary activities; and between their role as a party and as a movement. The 1983 elections demonstrated, however, that they are no longer a marginal and probably not a transitory phenomenon. Perhaps 10 percent of the electorate sympathizes with them. Some 50 to 60 percent is evidently with them in opposition to nuclear missiles and in support of stronger environmental legislation. Their insistence on broader and more varied political participation also has substantial appeal. They have now been legitimated by the voters, are making good use of their platforms in the legislatures to broaden their appeal, and have come into a share of those public monies paid out to all parties with substantial followings. As new, less traditional attitudes spread in German society, the Greens stand a good chance of capitalizing upon them to fortify their position and become a fixture in German politics.

WHAT DECIDED THE ELECTION?

Issues pushed by the Greens were of secondary or tertiary importance in the election outcome, however. Economics dominated, all analysts agree. Ever neurotic about the state of their economy, only 20 percent of Germans polled just before the election felt optimistic about the country's economic prospects. Differences over economic policy had brought the SPD/FDP coalition down in October, with the Liberals posing increasingly as defenders of the economic interests of the middle classes and demanding drastic cuts in social welfare benefits, new tax policies to stimulate business investment, and a more deflationary economic policy—a program that neither the SPD left nor the most powerful trade unions could accept.

Simply put, the voters' decision was to let the "outs" try out their remedies for the country's economic problems. A highly indicative poll late in the winter showed that half the public believed that the CDU could deal better even with unemployment than could the Social Democrats, who, like left parties everywhere, had always made joblessness their particular issue. Using its slogan "Vote for Recovery," the CDU ran a smooth, effective campaign to exploit the previous government's economic failings. It was aided by the fact that early signs of recovery were already evident in January and February. Kohl's party was thus in the happy position of not being seen as incumbents, although it had been in formal power since October's coalition shuffle, and at the same time being able to associate itself with the incipient upswing.

The SPD not only suffered from being the party of incumbency, it also positioned itself poorly and ran an inept campaign. The refusal of the popular Schmidt to lead his party again raised questions in voters' minds about conditions within the party. The candidacy of Vogel, a Catholic and Southern German, the first ever to head the SPD, was calculated to preserve the safe and sane image which Schmidt had given the party. But Vogel was less well known than Kohl, had little time to project himself to the electorate, and equivocated on the question of whether the SPD would be ready to enter a coalition with the Greens. Probably the SPD was doomed from the outset to lose—although it need not have lost so badly. Since it has never been within striking distance of an absolute majority, voters asked themselves whom it would choose as its eventual coalition partner. Not the FDP, from which it had just parted company. Not the CDU/CSU, which seemed victory-bound. The Greens? That option was unsettling to the basically conservative German electorate.

Deployment of the American missiles, the Pershing and cruise, also ranked high on the voters' agenda, although far below economic problems such as unemployment, inflation and government deficits, and even below environmental protection. The Christian Democrats were masterful in converting the missile issue into a test of loyalty to the Americans and the Atlantic alliance. The SPD may also have been damaged by Soviet public statements which Kohl's party interpreted as publicly indicating that Moscow favored the Social Democrats. On the other hand, White House backing of the CDU, which was obvious although never explicit, probably proved beneficial to Kohl.

A WATERSHED

Trends revealed in the 1983 election results will be long-lasting, given the glacial pace of political change in the Federal Republic. Some analysts were quick to classify Helmut Kohl's victory as swelling a conservative wave which, started by Margaret Thatcher and Ronald Reagan, was now reaching German shores. Those who interpret it as a ringing reaffirmation for centrism look closer to the mark. By voting the Liberals in and keeping Strauss out, the German electorate surely intended to provide a check to conservative inclinations. Kohl himself is closer to the socially conscious traditions of the prewar Catholic Center party than to populist rightism represented by the CSU. And the workers who flocked to the Christian Democrats did not do so because they favored a German version of monetarism, supply-side economics, or muscular and costly defense policies.

Still over the next few years Germany will, under the Kohl government, be moving toward more conservative economic policies, with reductions in welfare-state spending, and toward a more robust assertion of national interests, particularly with the Soviet Union but also, at least in economic matters, with the United States. The relative weakness of the liberal FDP and the strength of the CSU within the cabinet has tipped the balance toward the right.

For some time to come the SPD will remain weak and unable to mount effective opposition. It faces the massive task of rebuilding from the bottom up and of regaining its hold on the cities and towns. Vogel has yet to prove himself a leader with the authoritative and popular appeal of a Brandt or Schmidt. Until he does the suspicion will remain that he bears a closer resemblance to the highly competent but essentially colorless SPD leaders of the 1950s, Eric Ollenhauer and Fritz Erler.

How much lasting significance should be attached to the emergence of the Greens? It is difficult to reconcile the strong endorsement of a CDU/CSU dominance with the surprising success of the subculture-based Greens. The small party's success constitutes a warning that the political system must be more responsive to changes in society that have taken place over the past decade and to new issues that these changes bring to the fore. Dealing with the Greens will force the three established parties to confront these issues, introducing new dynamism into German politics. The success also injects new plebiscitary and populist elements into the system and an American-style readiness to practice politics outside as well as through the traditional parties. The vote for stability represented by the CDU/CSU victory and for change indicated by the Greens' success together suggest a combination of stability and dynamism that will reinforce democracy in the Federal Republic.

At first glance the 1983 elections seem to have restored a political landscape of the 1950s: a dominant CDU/CSU, a weak SPD, and several minor parties. Chancellor Kohl enjoys promoting this impression by referring to himself as the heir of Konrad Adenauer. Citizens of the Federal Republic in 1983, however, are vastly more self-confident, more experienced in democratic politics and more respected abroad. More of them today than in the 1950s are ready on their own to question national security policies. Such public involvement with foreign policy is an inevitable result of that trend toward greater democracy which the United States has welcomed ever since it started to play an active role in Germany's affairs nearly forty years ago.

CONTRIBUTORS

ROBERT GERALD LIVINGSTON is Acting Director of the American Institute for Contemporary German Studies, The Johns Hopkins University. He was formerly President of the German Marshall Fund of the United States.

CATHERINE McARDLE KELLEHER is Professor and Director of National Security Studies at the School of Public Affairs, University of Maryland.

ANGELA E. STENT is Associate Professor, Government Department, Georgetown University, and Research Associate, The Georgetown Center for Strategic and International Studies.

STEPHEN F. SZABO is Professor for National Security Affairs, The National Defense University, Washington, D.C., and Professional Lecturer in European Studies, School of Advanced International Studies, The Johns Hopkins University.